Memories Of
The Lockdown Years
4th Book in the 'Memories' series

Copyright © 2026 Rosanne Gallagher

All rights reserved. No part of this publication may be reproduced or transmitted in any form or by any means, electronic or mechanical including photocopying, recording or any information storage or retrieval system, without prior permission in writing from the publishers.

The right of Rosanna Gallagher to be identified as the author of this work has been asserted by her in accordance with the Copyright, Designs and Patents Act 1988

First published in the United Kingdom in 2026 by
The Choir Press

ISBN: 978-1-78963-598-0

Cover design by Bob Hellyer
www.BobHellyer.art
Typeset by Phoenix Media
www.phoenixmediadesign.com

"Thank you to my wonderful family and friends – without all of you there would be no book"

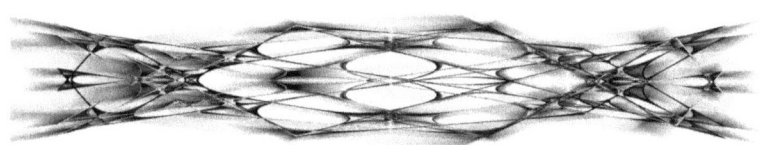

The following information from the UK government website:

'As of 19 March 2020 COVID-19 is no longer considered to be a High Consequence Infectious Disease (HCID) in the U.K.'

The country locked down on 23 March 2020

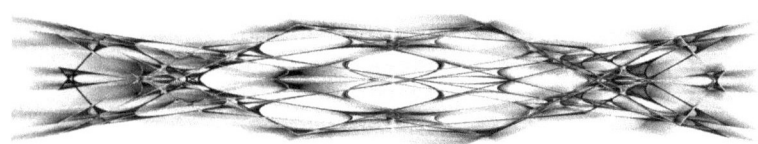

Introduction

Hello again - it's hard to believe two years have gone by... it's great to be back!

When I planned the trilogy back in 2021, I thought that a trilogy set over a three year period, would see us nicely through whatever needed to be sorted out in the world after covid started in 2020.

I was wrong and I realise that. I now realise the magnitude of what we are going through, or do I? Probably not, indeed I think that none of us really know.

I spent the winter of 2023/2024 deliberating and considering what I was going to write next... I had lots of ideas and some great suggestions came my way, but, as the months went by I received overwhelming encouragement and pursuasion from friends and people around the world, to continue collecting the stories of ordinary people over these years, and so I have!

A lot has happened in the last two years!

As you read through, you will see that some of my wonderful writers from Books 1, 2 and 3, have joined me again in this sequel to the original trilogy, and some have not. All of them did a fabulous job over those three years giving their perspectives and telling us about their experiences for which I will be forever grateful.

I welcome some lovely new writers with their unique stories and I hope you'll enjoy Book 4 as much as I have, as ever, hearing new views, opinions and heartfelt experiences illustrating that "We don't all see things the same way."

I am thinking there will be a continuation next year, and the year after that, and the next one, and the next one, as we watch our world unfold.

Please enjoy the stories and information that I've included in this book and I'll look forward to seeing you again at the end...

'It's All About The Children'

Rosanne

The autumn of 2023 was the same as the previous two autumns, editing around the clock to prepare Book 3, the final book of the 'Memories of Lockdown' trilogy, to send off to my publisher. All the work, all the excitement of the final decisions and all the fears of what could go wrong!

We've been through two English winters since I last wrote, filled with the dreary, grey, cool and cold days, sometimes rain and occasional snow, and with bright, blue-sky, sunny days, which my Dad would call 'Champagne Days' - he was right - those magical days, often unexpected, which make them even more fabulous!

Christmases filled with family, friends and walking dogs, eating too much and generally enjoying... the usual stuff! Shops and streets filled with Christmas lights and goodies, the infectious excitement of the children, the Christmas carols which I love to hear, and then, just like that, it's January, that long month when we all dream of Spring and those longer, lighter days!

The New Year of 2024 saw many grey skies and rain, lots of rain - poor people in the flooded areas and poor farmers! People displaced as their homes flooded, and cows and sheep huddled together on the higher land untill the water subsided. Driving anywhere was a challenge and fields turned into sparkling lakes!

Rosanne

At the end of March 2024 our beautiful dog 'Onyx' passed and it was very sad. He had followed Joe from Spain to England in 2020, but as life got busier for Joe, Onny spent more and more time with me and I adored him.

'My Tribute to Onny'
In 2008 a beautiful black puppy was abandoned outside our home in Spain; it was a hot day in early September and we were having a late afternoon swim, when we heard the screeching of brakes as a car pulled up, stopped briefly, a door opened and closed, then the car sped off. Onny had been dumped!

We ran out into the road and there he was, a young puppy, probably six months old, adorable and irresistable; we didn't know then how this confused little puppy dog would become such a huge and precious part of our lives! He moved in and spent the next six months eating all our shoes, and the next 16 years eating practically anything his nose came across!

In his last year he became very deaf and quite blind. When he could no longer jump in and out of the car, we walked locally, and when he could no longer walk upstairs, we slept downstairs. He was never alone.

When it became clear it was 'time to say goodbye', he died at home in my arms surrounded by family. Darling boy - so very special and still with us in our hearts and on our walks, "And Onny, we still watch out for our food on a low table in case you get there before us!! Ha Ha!"

He had had a wonderful life, but that didn't make it any easier to say goodbye. Thank you Sarah for your gentle care and support, to guide us through our final farewell xx

The winters can seem long, but each season has it's magic, and the winters lead us into spring with the new hope it brings each year, and longer, lighter days.

Spring had arrived and after Onny passed, it was time for me to move again; it felt hard leaving the house where he'd lived with us, but by June I was ready to go!

I had so much help with my move from my son Joe, and friends, but I hadn't anticipated how exhausting it would be physically and emotionally!

So much sorting, the rediscovery of so many memories in cards and photos, and many other personal things.

However, after leaving the old house I found myself very happy in my new home - it was just what I needed!

The summer of 2024 was spent settling in, exploring local walks, meeting my lovely new neighbours and generally starting to feel 'at home' - it felt good!

We had an early summer that year, with some beautiful hot days, but by the beginning of July the sun had left us and by September we found ourselves heading into autumn, feeling we had not had much of a summer at all. The bit of sunshine we had had, seemed long ago!

A new home, and in the sorting out, settling in period, I found myself reflecting on the previous years, the previous summers...

Rosanne

I remembered the last summer I spent with my parents at the family home in 2019...

When Dad couldn't water his precious flowers and lawn any more, we did it together, slowly moving his walking frame around, trying not to get tangled up with the water hose... we laughed amidst the frustration of it all and he never complained, he only gave thanks. Each night we'd sit on his bed together and he'd joke about how all the routine things he had whizzed through all his life, now took such a long time to do and were hard work, but we found a way and at least we did it together.

Mum found her way through her discomforts and frustrations during that last year, without complaint, and still always looking out for Dad. What amazing people - how lucky I am to have such parents.

Above all, the wonderful conversations we shared, much reminiscing over times we'd spent together, and stories of times in their past. Very special.

Having said goodbye to Mum and Dad in the last years, I have found myself adjusting to life in a world where I am no longer a child. The realisation that my age was irrelevant, the fact that I had children and grandchildren of my own; none of that altered the fact that my parents were physically gone and nothing was the same any more.

Even as adults, we desperately miss turning to the unconditional love of our parents until we realise they're always with us; I turn to them daily for advice and I receive it - they still help me find my way!

*'forever forget-me-nots
- Fieldings'*

During those last years we became so close... I wanted to protect them from everything... unfortunately I couldn't, and that was the harshest lesson of all. However, through the 'not much fun' times we shared laughter, lots of it, and at the strangest and often most difficult moments!

One night I heard a thump and leapt out of bed thinking one of them had fallen... Mum had heard the same and we practically collided on the landing, racing towards Dad's room. There he was on the floor, where we joined him! Fortunately he wasn't hurt, but he couldn't get himself back up into bed, and Mum and I couldn't immediately think of a way to get him back into bed. So we sat there, in the middle of the night, on the floor, and we laughed at our predicament! We eventually found a way, but how wonderful it was to have been able to laugh at a moment like that!

The day Mum collapsed going from her room to the bathroom, I tried to catch her and we both ended up on the floor! Neither of us were hurt and we laughed until we had the energy to get back up again!

And so many other situations which were awful, but somehow we managed to see the funny side!
I wouldn't have missed a single moment!

Life goes on, and often I hear myself sounding like one of my parents, which makes me smile with happiness and a sense of belonging, it reminds me how near they are to me at every step. 💜

In previous books I have spoken of the PHA (People's Health Alliance) - a project I co-organise in Glastonbury. The aim is to share knowledge and information about alternative health options so that people can make well-informed decisions for their own health, and for the health of their loved ones.

We meet every fortnight to discuss, and we regularly invite Speakers to talk to us about what they offer, including Frequency Energy Healing, Homeopathy and Flower Essences, Reiki, Reflexology, End of Life Care and Grief, Pain Free Healing. It also serves as a wonderful way of bringing people together!

I have also spoken of the 'Energy Enhancement System' based on Frequency Energy Healing and how a group of us were determined to have a Healing Centre here in Glastonbury. I am thrilled to say that the right people came along who were able to make the dream come true, and have opened their doors.

In March 2024, I was asked to organise an Event in Glastonbury with three Speakers and an audience of around 100 people. It was a 'sold out' Event, a great evening and led to others, all of which have been equally enjoyable and successful.

It reminded me that I have always been passionate about the importance of people's voices being heard, people sharing their very different knowledge and opinions, which is of course the very theme of my 'Memories' trilogy and this book. "We don't all see things the same way."

In May 2025 I was planning an Event in Glastonbury... it was cancelled three times! Cancelled by the Town Hall and St John's church and the only other venue big enough for our Event was The Assembly Rooms, and they weren't interested in our booking. We were being censored here in Glastonbury, known across the world for welcoming diversity. We then booked the village hall in nearby Compton Dundon, and they cancelled us 4 days before the Event.

No-one at the venues who cancelled us took the time to look into the few objections - all very disappointing and the ugly realisation was that we do not have Freedom of Speech in Glastonbury. A small reflection of what is going on across the UK and the world!

We eventually held the Event in a beautiful smallholding nearby.

We enjoyed a day full of sunshine - the numbers attending the Event had grown, and we were surrounded by lovely people keen to support Freedom of Speech.

A light always shines through adversity and in this case, two lights shone brightly. The first was the light that shone on Glastonbury, highlighting its censorship which people across the world were, and will be shocked at. The light that shone for me personally, was the incredible support I received from the ticket holders who never gave up on the Event; they stuck with us through the three cancellations and almost all of them managed to get to the fourth-time arranged Event.

They trusted me with their ticket money over a four month period while we went from one cancellation to another. They encouraged me at every step of the way - those who thought of my personal journey and in practical terms, the stress and expenses I incurred along the way - kind, amazing people! I couldn't have done it without them. 'Collectively we made it happen!'

On the day of the Event, I took the opportunity to grab the microphone and thank everyone, it was very emotional and it reminded me how important it is to choose carefully those we spend time with, work with, play with, the importance to always choose those who make us feel  good, appreciate us and whose words and actions are uplifting! That's what I took away with me from this experience!
I received such kindness.
Let's always remember to be kind to each other.'

Something I remember my Dad telling me many years ago...
'The measure of the man is shown in times of adversity. That is the time when you recognise those who support you, and you choose who you want walking by your side.'

Freedom of Speech being challenged... how important is it to you?
"Ultimately, arguing that you don't care about the right to privacy because you have nothing to hide, is no different than saying you don't care about free speech because you have nothing to say."
Edward Snowden

Throughout our existence we have fought physically for our freedom, but personally I do not choose to stay on that never-ending treadmill which only prospers the few who instigated it in the first place.
No.
Enough is Enough.
All I want is peace.

I no longer support this side or that side,
I just want the fighting to stop.

We just need to say 'No' and it stops.

Wars being funded with taxpayers money. Do we want wars? No. Were we asked if we wanted our money to pay for wars? Who profits from wars? It's time for each and every one of us to decide whether we want wars and division as part of our lives going forward, or break the pattern and create a peaceful world where we thrive, not just survive. It's time to 'Restore the Balance.'

In the words of Barclay James Harvest's 'Child of the Universe'. (1974)
Please lay down your pistols and your rifles
Please lay down your colours and your creeds
Please lay down your thoughts of being no-one
Concentrate on what you ought to be
Then lay down your bullshit and your protests
Then lay down your governments of greed
Take a look at what lies all around you
Then pray God we can live in peace

When traditional systems collapse
Alternative solutions are born

Something I've discussed with many over the past months is how we are watching the old systems fall, they don't serve us now, and haven't for a very long time. The old play is coming to an end, the final scenes are playing out, we see the actors shouting louder and louder as fewer and fewer people are listening to them any more. Many have had enough of the current protagonists and their script which only benefits them.

The new play is the change of the world, and the way we choose to live is unfolding. The new play has already begun and a lot of structure is already in place. The world is changing before our eyes, if our eyes are open to see; it's all happening very fast and this time WE are making the choices, choosing carefully the changes we make. Choose your Frequency!

We recognise that we are all connected, everything is energy and a sense of Unity is being restored as we remember. It's like a jigsaw and we are the pieces; we all have an important part to play in completing the puzzle, and in doing so, we recover our communities from the grassroots up and we build and rebuild the systems that are important to us in a way that will benefit us, and our needs.

Even though the nightly news and every headline in every newspaper depicts horror and division, a world in absolute chaos, and indeed there is much division and chaos, we have no idea what is true and what is not true. I believe there is a much bigger positive picture, bigger than we could imagine!

It doesn't matter who is right or wrong, the important thing is that more and more people across the world want Peace and Unity, and that's what we are creating as we go forward each day in our different ways.

The last years have been a series of 'endings and new beginnings' for me and I realised very early on, that yearning for anyone or anything that was no longer in my life, was not going to help me create a new life here in England.

I have enjoyed building my new life, creating new traditions, finding new friends, discovering new places, walking barefoot in the Abbey gardens, driving to the sea to feel the sand under my feet, and going forward with my children and grandchildren... discovering new opportunities, which ten years ago I could never have imagined - it's been a wonderful new adventure!

Taking every day as it comes, enjoying the blue skies of today and looking forward to the even bluer skies of tomorrow. Remembering... 'it's all exactly as it's meant to be and I will always live in wonderment and love... forever optimistic'. 💜

"Wonderment & Love"

Víctor Hernández

When I was faced with a blank page to write these first lines, I had to have a serious talk with myself. Hey! Don't stress yourself and don't procrastinate the completion of this text. It is impossible to summarize such an intense period in a few pages. So, I will give you an overview of my experience, highlighting what transformed me most from this experience and the conclusions of what it has given me to grow as a human being.

The Blindfold
In Spain, I frequently watch English news from CNN, BBC, NHK. I remember watching the news the day that the 34-year-old ophthalmologist Li Wenliang passed away. After the same doctor reported pneumonia of unknown origin in Wuhan, he was reprimanded by the police for 'spreading false information'. He died two months later after being disconnected from a ventilator.

We are all familiar with what follows from the continuous bombardment of information we were subjected to.

One issue that really caught my attention was the lack of interest paid to that strange pneumonia during the following weeks. The government and social media were not really concerned in spreading the information about the virus.

I am not a doctor, I am a veterinarian, but it is not difficult to understand that a contagious disease that is transmitted - among other ways - through the air, is today in China and tomorrow in any part of the world. Diseases, as we know, do not understand borders and even less in a globalized world.

In Spain we went through several phases: passivity from the politicians, a phase of alertness concerning deaths and hysteria due to the fact of an unknown disease that had to be tackled as soon as possible.

Globally we suffered the confinement with some measures being logical, and others somewhat absurd. Then came the vaccine and then oblivion.

Masks and Vaccines

Masks were one of the most complicated issues for me. In social and work spaces it made sense to wear them. However, in outdoor spaces, when you didn't come across anyone or when we were later allowed to go out in nature, I thought it made no sense. Will I get Covid-19 from a tree or a stone? The worst thing was not being able to breathe fresh air and to see the children wearing masks. The little angels soon got used to it and didn't protest, but it was overwhelming for parents. It was the sensible thing to do to try to reduce the spread of the disease, but it was a preventive patch that did not stop the spread. So science began to look for solutions at an accelerated pace until the discovery of new vaccines. Some leaders, such as Trump, recommended drinking water with bleach... This man may know a lot about economics, but he has never opened a book on biology in his life. Nothing new, a rich man with little culture can be president of the USA, but a wise man without being a millionaire could never be one. In the end, it is the American population whom allow themselves to be deceived.

What about the vaccine? This was a very controversial issue that seems to have passed into history. I sensed at the time that it would shape a division of society into vaccinated and unvaccinated. Shortly before patenting the first messenger RNA-type Covid vaccines, Anthony Fauci had said that such vaccines would take many years to develop, and that they were not safe because it would take several years to prove their efficiency and safety. Within a few months, when progress was close to approving the first vaccines, not only were they declared to be safe and effective by Fauci, but vaccination was recommended for all ages.

In my case, after reading a lot of scientific literature and watching interviews with different doctors, I decided not to vaccinate myself and also to avoid vaccinating my 9-year-old daughter. Her mother also agreed with this decision. We made this decision because after observing the statistics for several months, children were not seriously affected. There had been no deaths in children. To summarize a lot, it was a disease that mostly ravaged immunocompromised and elderly people, and occasionally in middle-aged people, but not in children. Moreover, after such scientific readings it was concluded that unvaccinated people were not more transmissible than vaccinated people. Therefore, given my ethical doubts about not being a risk to third parties, I decided that the choice to vaccinate or not to vaccinate should be a free choice. And above all, the most important thing was to protect children.

The people, pressured by politicians and by the surrealistic situation, dramatically changed their behaviour. Even families stopped talking to you if you didn't get vaccinated. When news of side effects appeared, people generally looked the other way and heard that this happens with all medicines. We went from a time when people were generally very critical of the Spanish political class, to a phase of 'I'm going to do whatever you ask me because I'm afraid'. It was not a legal obligation to get vaccinated, but a social obligation. Today, hundreds of people claiming for the side effects and after-effects of life-long vaccinations, have been told by the government that 'they freely chose to be vaccinated'…

With regard to vaccination, many questions remained unanswered. I asked doctors and they did not have answers to some of my questions. Today many remain unanswered, but very few people are currently vaccinated annually against Covid. A lot of people believe that the that Covid-19 transformed into a simple cold, but I keep asking myself, why has Covid 19 also ceased to be a problem in Africa and other regions of the world, where the vaccines were not or only partially distributed?

What actual side effects have occurred and which remain unresearched today?

Why were they revaccinated up to 4 or 5 times if they were recognized as effective from the beginning? Was it a trial-and-error?

Why were vaccine administrations from different pharmaceuticals mixed in Spain, without knowing the risk of that multiple and experimental vaccination?

Why is it that when compensation for side effects is asked for in Spain, the government now responds that every citizen voluntarily was vaccinated?

Are there actually any studies taking place on possible medium-term side effects in the vaccinated population?

Negative and fear
The most negative aspects of the pandemic period were obviously the deaths and their impact on families, the after-effects of the disease, the side-effects of the vaccines, the fear of illness and death and the uncertainty of not knowing how long this seemingly endless period would last.

Did this period bring anything positive?
Sure, even from the worst situations, glimmers of light can emerge. But let's face it, not everyone learns from their experiences. Most of humanity is back to business as usual. We are still immersed in wars and conflicts on every continent that seem to have no end. They are led by egomaniacs and selfish heads of state, whether for economic, expansionism, religious reasons, etc.

So, I believe more in the positive things that each human being or each family was able to extract from their own experience. Many people took this period as an impulse or turning point to improve their way of understanding life, or to increase their happiness as much as possible.

Personal and positive family experience
The most positive thing is that I have been able to enjoy many hours with my daughter, Daniela, who was 9-years-old in 2020. Before the pandemic when I was stuck in the loop of taking Daniela to school, coming back to work and then driving in 'taxi-mode' to take her to sport activities, the days were passing like dominoes. So, one positive thing it brought is to eliminate the daily stress of schedules and commuting.

During this period of confinement, we set up a home gym and exercised every day. We watched movies, played games, did homework, argued, forgave each other, cooked together, walked the dog and had many moments of conversation. Not all the time was ideal, but this experience taught us to stop, to look at things in a different way, to slowly escape from the rush and to value what is really important in  the day-to-day and in being alive. Besides, music was a privileged companion. So much so, that currently Daniela, 5 years later while we listen to the radio or playlists, says to me: "Listen daddy, our music of confinement." It remains as bittersweet music, because they were moments that fused sadness with joy.

The hardest part, no doubt, was trying to telework while Daniela was doing homework and pronouncing the word "daddy" every 2 minutes. The dog, 'Manchitas' on the other hand, looked at us with a pitiful face to take her for another walk. I don't think the little Jack Russell did that many miles in her life. I have to remember that for a few months we were only allowed to leave our home to walk the dog, for shopping, going to the bank or for medical visits.

Family and social networks
Nowadays we are saturated with WhatsApp and Telegram groups, life is not enough. But at that time, it was an escape route to be able to share experiences, worries and celebrations with friends and family. The positive side was, above all, to remember friends and family that we had forgotten a little over time. So, some friendships and family relationships were rescued and continue today.

I even discovered that I had a Pakistani neighbour in the townhouse next door, and we had very pleasant conversations. At 8pm we would look out to applaud the work of the sanitary workers, and I would bring out my African drum to liven up the applause, and his children were very amused to hear the rhythms I was playing.

Police adventures
The most fun and exciting things I remember, were my night-time escapades to do sports on the fringes of the law. I would climb over the walls of my townhouse, making sure beforehand that the police weren't patrolling. In a way I felt like I was escaping from Alcatraz. I would cross the street and hide in some hedges in case I heard a police car approaching. Once I got into a beautiful wetland with plenty of wild birds, called 'Clot de Galvany' in Gran Alacant, I felt free. Then I started to run through the nature between trees, lagoons and birds until I reached the sea. What a feeling!

I was alone on a paradisiacal beach, far away from the repetitive and negative news and with pure air to breathe. The air was purer than ever: air and car traffic were suspended. It was a paradox, but in the face of an unknown respiratory virus, outside our homes we were breathing the cleanest air possibly since the industrial revolution.

Taking up hobbies
After a few years of forgetting to study music, I took up percussion and guitar again. And since then, I haven't stopped. Now I'm getting into the wonderful world of Jazz with the drums and learning to play the piano. If we were to be 'locked up' again, my best friend would be the piano. I think my little 'Manchitas' would be jealous.

Learning to be with oneself and meditate

How difficult it is to spend time in silence with oneself. So many thoughts, sensations and feelings come to the surface in stillness and silence. So, another thing that I incorporated, were the meditations of Ramiro Calle, a very wise Spanish man who introduced Yoga in Spain in the 50s. On the other hand, I discovered among other readings, Eckhart Tolle and his book 'Power Of Now', through which I started to be more aware of the present and of each moment. The past and the future do not exist - he teaches in his book - the only thing we really have is the present moment. If you think about it carefully, it is true, the mind invents non-existent future movies and the past only remains in memories, videos and photographs, but it no longer exists.

From time to time, a cold beer or a glass of wine while watching a film was also a pleasure. But, as my father says, you always have to keep your vices under control.

Have we learnt anything? Final reflection

On an individual level I have learnt above all to appreciate every moment and every day. I have always enjoyed life and the wonderful things that miraculously exist. I didn't need a pandemic to become aware of this. But it is true that it did push me to further strengthen my personality and my bond with Daniela. I even met my current partner Clara, an excellent, kind and wonderful person, who was my neighbor at the time.

Now, even more so, I enjoy things intensely, to the point of having to stop sometimes to rest and sleep reluctantly. Nowadays, I don't allow anxious thoughts to invade me in the face of the fleetingness of life: today I have learnt and done this - I think like this every day - but I have left other things undone…

The important thing is quality, not quantity, and to choose well in what things you spend your time. And of course, what kind of people are worthwhile.

During the pandemic we couldn't choose, so now the key is to choose well and be humble: you can't read all the books in the world, see all the films, travel to every country, etc... what you can do is to choose well each step and above all, enjoy each activity and personal relationship to the maximum, without ever losing the illusion of living intensely. And accepting that not everything is always going to be beautiful and that in life, unpleasant things also happen. So, we have to debate between illusion and acceptance, making beautiful moments while we can, because the ugliest things like the pandemic come by themselves and without warning.

Let's live fully! And as my friend Janet Jackson - a wonderful person and artist who encouraged me to write these lines - would say, "**Always In Spirit**."

Clara

We live in strange times. We often watch the news and it feels like we're watching a movie, as if what appears on the screen isn't real. I suppose our brain doesn't have the capacity to process all the information we receive in such a short time. We are simply not programmed for that.

Surely, that's what happened to me when I first started hearing about COVID. 'I can't believe what's happening in China.' You never really believe that something like this will hit close to home. Although, despite the widespread blindness, there are always people who act as 'tribe guardians', people who are capable of seeing beyond.

Two days before they closed the schools and made us confine ourselves at home for more than 3 months, the moms from the music school where I taught called me to say they were scared. They didn't want their children to be exposed to that 'something' that no-one really knew what it was. When I informed the school owner that there would be no class the next day, she got angry. The numbers didn't add up for her that month, and she didn't see the risk that having class could pose for the little ones. Mothers and their sixth sense. Good thing they can see beyond.

Shortly after, we were locked up at home. I am not a fearful or hypochondriacal person, so I tried to organise my life and my family's life in the most normal way possible under the circumstances. My role as a mother was to try to ensure that my 5-year-old daughter, Valeria, was not aware of what was happening. She knew that as a precaution we shouldn't leave the house, but she never experienced it with fear or distress. In fact, we even enjoyed being able to have breakfast together every morning on the balcony before starting the day's tasks. Moreover, the temperature that spring was especially pleasant.

Every day, at 8pm we would go out onto the balcony to applaud the healthcare workers who were facing the virus, helping as best as they could. Afterwards, we would go back inside to prepare dinner and go to bed.

One day, after the applause, we decided to bring some speakers to the balcony and played about 10 minutes of music to cheer ourselves up. At first, people didn't react, but they stayed on their terraces listening. A few days later, we all knew each other, dancing on the balconies, and if necessary, we even sang 'Happy Birthday' to the lucky one of the day. It was our way of forgetting for a while what was happening and that was beyond our control. The way not to think about the fact that, that day, you had gone to the supermarket and it scared you just to think that you might have brought the virus home.

Clara

Even so, after those dances, I couldn't help but feel deeply sad. While everyone finished dancing, I used to hide on the kitchen terrace and look out the window. I felt completely alone. We are programmed to always look outward, to always have something to do. That 100-day pause meant a look inward into everyone's life. Of course, you know what works or doesn't in your life, but it's easy to ignore it when you don't have time to think about it. When you stop, the reality within you becomes more present, and you have no choice but to face it head-on.

With the arrival of summer, the lockdowns began to ease. It seemed that the pandemic was retreating, and the people's eagerness to return to normal life and the authority's desire to economically recover the country, suddenly opened the doors of the houses.

I still remember the first weekend of 'freedom'. We went to sleep at some friends place in the countryside with the kids. It was like a summer camp when you're a kid, really fun.

A few weeks later, we went to the beach house in Santa Pola and decided to stay there in case we had to lock ourselves up at home again. We had a large terrace, and the Clot de Galvany natural park with its lagoons was visible from the terrace. Everything was noisy again, and quickly Valeria found a gang of friends she wouldn't part with either day or night. The 'summer camp' again.

The neighbours downstairs, a guy in his 40s and his 10-year-old daughter, just moved in and quickly, we became friends. The girls got along perfectly and spent their time going up and down from one house to the other.

Everything seemed to be fine on the surface. However, I still felt the same sadness as during the lockdown. My marriage was ending. Many things had changed inside of me, despite everyone on the outside was trying to return to the way that things were before.

At the beginning of the new school year, the restrictions returned, and two days before my birthday, on November 5th, we were confined again. This time it caught us at the beach house, where we were going to celebrate, so I had to cancel the party with my friends. It was very strange. We ended up having dinner with the neighbours downstairs, whom we didn't know very well but were the only ones we could meet with (always on the terrace and outdoors, of course).

Sometimes bonds are not formed with those you choose, but with those who are close to you. And if everything flows naturally, you can't help but thank God for the fact that life smiles at you slightly in difficult times.

From that moment on, our day-to-day life became a game of dice. Each week, they would open or close access to the cities based on the declared COVID cases. Elche, the city where we had spent the first lockdown, was almost always closed, so we registered in Santa Pola, where we could move around freely. While all this was happening, the first news about the imminent production of COVID vaccines began to be heard. A good piece of news in concept, but there was a lot of contradictory information about it. Everyone comes from where they come from, and in my case, I come from a family of doctors and pharmacists.

Since I was little, I loved listening to the stories my grandfather, a healthcare professional, told about how his father prepared medicines in the pharmacy of the Monastery of Santo Domingo de Silos in Burgos. It always seemed to me that it must be something like making magic potions, and on several occasions, I visited the monastery to imagine my great-grandfather there. Many times I heard my grandfather say that a medication should never be considered good until it had been in the experimental phase for at least 10 years. These are the kinds of things you hear as a child and barely pay attention to.

However, the day I heard on the news that they were developing several vaccines and that in a few months they wanted to administer them to millions of people, that phrase dormant in the back of my mind resurfaced. Then I thought: 'I'm not going to take it. I have it clear'. It was as if my grandfather was protecting me from Heaven.

At first, it was just an intuition, but as time went by, it became a firm conviction. My downstairs neighbour, a veterinarian by profession, heard me talking about this one day. At first, he looked at me with surprise. Then, his intelligent eyes sparkled as if he had discovered a treasure. Obviously, he had much more scientific knowledge than I did, so he started researching vaccines, not only through the Spanish press but also by looking for international news. He also spoke with doctors and veterinarian friends who lived in different countries.

The world was divided. I'm not referring to the people on the street who are very easy to manipulate through the media, fuelling hatred towards those who think differently, but rather to the world of medicine. There was an official scientific section that supported the pharmaceutical companies, and another that was silenced because it spoke about the danger of treating so many people with an experimental drug.

Everyone's intention was good, they wanted to help people, but from different perspectives. In my case, this was not a dilemma; I was very clear about what I was going to do, and fortunately, my closest family supported me. What I found curious was analysing the social experiment that was being carried out.

I perfectly understand that when there is a problem, solutions must be sought, and that is what the vaccine represented for many, but behind those good intentions, there were many other interests. I had the feeling that some of these interests were not clearly visible due to people's fear. Fear, that enormous monster that gives you the power to manipulate people.

The first doses of the vaccine arrived, initially only for adults, and it seems that 'almost everyone' received it with joy. But more people than expected refused to get 'the vaccine they were assigned'. The government then decided to create strong social pressure to force them to get it even against their will - 'If you don't get the vaccine, you can't enter restaurants. If you don't get the vaccine, I won't hire you. If you don't get the vaccine, you can't travel to certain countries'. Of course, the vaccine was 'voluntary'. The aim was to ensure that everyone got vaccinated without having judicial responsibilities for what might happen afterwards.

To all this, we must add family pressures. Christmas was approaching, and not being vaccinated was little more than being an outcast. Somebody from my family even told me: "If something happens to us because of you, don't talk to me anymore." The best part of all is that many of those people who were supposed to be civic-minded for getting vaccinated, were later seen without masks in crowded bars and restaurants.

During the pandemic, I avoided crowds at all times and of course, I never took off my mask in places where there were people. In reality, I rarely found myself in crowds. Our weekend entertainment used to be going to the mountains, where we could breathe in the fresh air without hardly running into anyone.

What those days did serve for, was to make me realise how the people around me were really like. I found doctors who believed in the vaccine, but never judged me for not getting vaccinated. Also, those who had no scientific knowledge but attacked me for avoiding the unknown side effects of the vaccine, while COVID severity incidence in young people was minimal.

I had my ideas, but I never tried to impose them on anyone; that's why I also didn't understand that others wanted to impose theirs on me.

After the vaccination of adults, the children's vaccination came, and the problems it caused among peers with differing ideas about whether or not to vaccinate their children. Fortunately, that was not my case. My now ex-husband and I were in complete agreement that we were not going to vaccinate our daughter.

Nowadays, I look back and try to see things clearly. I see the moments of uncertainty and fear, the people who died or were seriously ill from COVID, I see all those who couldn't say goodbye to their loved ones due to the state of alarm (myself included), the lack of information, the non-humanity of those who took advantage of the circumstances economically, and how easy it is to manipulate the masses through fear.

In those moments of crisis when everything around you seems to go crazy, what matters is not what is happening around you, but the decisions you make to face it.

After all this time, I think about my daughter, how she experienced it at the age of 5, being aware that something was happening, but overcoming the fear thanks to the work her father and I did. I think about the decision not to vaccinate ourselves, which of course involved a risk, and that today frees us from the fear of all those unknown side effects at that time. Now, many of them are well known.

I think about the strength of spirit we were able to demonstrate by being consistent with our convictions and respectful of those of others. And I feel proud. It's not about winning or knowing who's right, it's about being consistent.

After my divorce, someone accompanied me in these reflections. The downstairs neighbour, Víctor, who had looked at me with his intelligent eyes as if he discovered a treasure, and who thought that being honest with oneself was the most important thing one could do in life. Today, he is the person with whom I share my life.

We live in strange times, but sometimes, every now and then, a light appears that shows us the way. You just have to know how to see it and thank God for it.

LOVE

*"Follow your Heart
Let the Light Lead Through the Darkness
Back to a Place you Once Knew..."*

Brenda

It's hard to believe it is five years since covid and lockdown.

We tend to say before or after covid, it has become a major turning point in time. It certainly has made us reassess our lives, learning and appreciating what is important, realising what our priorities are.

Lots of people enjoyed the time of isolation, the freedom and time to think, meditate, learn and heal. I believe we learned more about ourselves.

We were brainwashed into feeling fear, completely out of proportion to the situation, the fear drove people to be vaccinated without reason.

Most people I know who were vaccinated now regret the decision, and would not have another. It is a personal decision, but at last people are asking questions. Since covid there has been an unusually high proportion of deaths, mostly without a reason or labelled as 'Sudden Death Syndrome'.

Recently here in Spain, we had a blackout, which caused complete chaos and disruption, particularly in busy areas.

Trains, the metro, electric vehicles and traffic lights stopped working, ATMs stopped working and businesses were unable to take card payments, Some homes were without water due to water pumps not working. Mobile phone networks failed and some stranded people suffered panic attacks. The emergency services were badly affected.

In my village we were fortunate as it was a local fiesta, and people who would normally have been travelling to work and school were at home instead. People went to the local bars, but had to scramble around to find cash to pay.

I always have some cash and so I chose a book, made my way across the road to the bar opposite, where I settled down with a glass of wine and my book and chatted to neighbours and friends as they came and went.

Everybody said it reminded them of the start of lockdown five years ago, it triggered the same feelings, that loss of freedom to do usual things and the fear of losing control. We were given an explanation of what happened, but some people still feel it was orchestrated.

Those of you who have read my previous stories, know that I am a Psychic Medium and I have spent a good deal of my professional life helping people through their fears over the past years. I have talked about people reassessing their lives and indeed I have witnessed the journey's of some of my clients making huge changes in their work, their relationships and every aspect of their lives; making painful decisions because they knew they had to go through the pain to get to where they wanted to be.

Perhaps the lesson we learn from the covid years is not to be controlled by fear, not be afraid to speak out, and, above all, to **'maintain personal choice'**.

Helen

As a child, although our family didn't have a dog or a cat or a pony I found a way to connect and spend time with animals; this was my joy and my escapism!

I knew a local farmer who let me ride his ponies and I had friends with dogs that I would walk or borrow. Cats were out and about so I could easily stop and chat to cats and I would sit on a golf course near my home and watch the rabbits playing.

I have always known animals are sentient beings and have often been treated very badly by us humans.

Over the years some beautiful animals shared my life and the lives of my children.

When my daughter was about 19 years old, 'Herbie', a little New Forest pony came to live with us; he was a cheeky character and taught me how to look after him.

I wanted a friend for Herbie and looking through 'Horse World' I found 'Bessie'. She was unwell and unwanted, but the moment I saw her I knew I wanted her and with patience and therapy from a wonderful woman I met at that time, she was cured and lived happily with me for 5 years working with the RDA (Riding for the Disabled) amongst the many other activities we shared together. She was very special to me and Herbie loved her so much. When she died Herbie died within weeks.

By this time I had bought a piece of land and now found myself with land but without horses, so I started to look through 'Horse World' again searching for horses who needed a home.

Almost immediately I found 'Toby'.

No-one wanted Toby, he was always dribbling and no-one had found a cure for him.

I spent my time sitting in the field with him, loving him and he stopped dribbling within weeks. I rode him until he didn't want to be ridden anymore, then he enjoyed a quiet life.

Then along came Kelly, a beautiful chestnut mare, joined shortly after by the very tall handsome strong 'Earl'.

Mission accomplished - I had filled my land with beautiful horses and I enjoyed these years so much.

Thinking back to the Spring of 2020... I was living in a small village in Somerset with my son, Dan, 22. and that was when we first heard of covid; we saw people dropping dead on the streets of Wuhan on the nightly news - the days when I used to watch the news! I can remember thinking 'Oh my God - we're all going to die' and everyone around me thought the same initially. I was in shock!

As the days and weeks went by, talking about it with my family, we all felt sorry for the people in Wuhan but thought 'It's never going to come here'.

I was working as a private 'Carer' and as the weeks went by we started to hear talk of a 'Lockdown'. We then saw the closing down of the schools, universities and many work places. The families of my elderly clients, in many cases, became the 'carers' and didn't want me in and out of their homes for risk of infection. I was only needed where there was no family; my workload was halved.

I continued to work, in and out of people's homes daily. One of my friends lived alone so we would meet for secret picnics in the fresh air; she worked in a care home, often on 12 hour shifts wearing a mask, so it was very important for her to get into the fresh air, and it made absolutely no sense not to. At this time, nurses would still attend the elderly if absolutely essential, although they would do as little 'hands-on' work as possible.

I received messages and directions from Somerset Council to go and collect PPE (Personal Protective Equipment) - masks, gloves, aprons and anti-bacterial handwash and when travel was banned, I was issued with a letter from the Council authorising me to drive around the local area. I enjoyed driving around as there was no traffic and no-one ever asked to see this authorisation letter.

My son, Dan, aged 22, and I worked at the Glastonbury Festival each year and were really looking forward to it, but as we started to hear of big crowd events being cancelled, I do remember wondering if the Festival would be cancelled.

It was - we were gutted.

It appeared that the only big event which carried on regardless was the Cheltenham Races in March 2020, just before Lockdown; we were surprised when we heard on the News that it would go ahead.

I had a conversation with one of the local farmers who told me he and a group of friends were going to the Races; I then heard they'd all caught covid at the Races and they were all ill. The farmer I'd spoken to was in hospital on a ventilator and a few days later he died; he had been a fit, healthy farmer in his 50s, it was very sad. The rest of his friends recovered but after his death everyone in the village was terrified.

I was watching news of empty hospitals and the videos of doctors and nurses dancing. Every Thursday night at 6pm everyone was encouraged to go out onto their doorstep and clap and cheer for the NHS. I did it for a couple of weeks and then it felt empty - it didn't make sense.

I enjoyed Lockdown - beautiful weather - lots of time with Dan, lovely walks - lots of cooking - sitting in the garden - growing vegetables - watched some Netflix and I even learnt how to 'game' with Dan!

Helen

Walking with Sparky and Skye... Sparky had been with me for over 12 years, he was a small jack russell cross and was beginning to show his age which was partly why Skye came to us, as I loved long walks and Sparky wasn't keen any more. Sadly Sparky decided it was his time to leave us in May 2020.

On arrival at the vet Dan and I were asked to wait outside the building with Sparky in our arms, we were then asked to hand him over but we refused as we knew we would never see him again - we wanted and needed to stay with him till the end. After a bit of resistance the vet allowed us to be with him.

Skye is a lurcher and she came to live with us, aged 7, in December 2019 - she and I enjoyed many long walks through the beautiful countryside all around us, and we still do.

During the first Lockdown our three cats, Bandit, Dusty and Sunny, walked out with me, Dan and the dogs. Our beautiful 4 year old Sunny loved these walks but unfortunately he was run over that summer when the roads became busy again. Bandit and Dusty are still with us and still walking out!

My older daughter, Lorna, and her children lived nearby and we saw a lot of them which was lovely; we walked and made the most of all the extra time together - the time Lockdown gave us with my work halved and my daughter and grandchildren with no work and no school!

All the gyms, swimming pools and wellness centres were closed and yet the fast food restaurants and off-licences stayed open -

it didn't make much sense to me to shut anything healthy but keep the drink and junk food available in a worldwide pandemic. Meanwhile the evening News reported on the daily covid death toll, never a word of hope.

Boris Johnson, Chris Whitty and Matt Hancock would appear, 'Next Slide Please' - deaths of people who had died in car accidents were added to the covid death toll if they had died within a certain amount of days of testing positive for covid. We were told to accept the scientific evidence of the 'experts' though it was obvious to me that things were not adding up - experts or no experts. Doctors across the world were beginning to express their fears about the information that was being fed to us via the media; they were silenced and reported as giving out 'misinformation'. Anyone who had an opinion that opposed the 'government/media' narrative was vilified, deplatformed, and labelled as a conspiracy theorist.

Somewhere along the way I stumbled across the UK Column News and from then on that was the only news programme I took any notice of. As I listened I found it all making much more sense to me - I stopped listening to the BBC News. I kept up to date and informed of the headlines, but it hadn't made any sense to me for too long.

I remember the traffic light system at the doors of supermarkets so that only a certain number of people were in the store at any one time, and one way systems round the store... not being able to stop for too long and a crime to speak anyone.

On the rare occasion I was stopped and asked to put a mask on, I always said politely "No thank you." I picked up an 'exempt' lanyard and kept it on me in case I was asked though I chose not to wear it.

Helen

I thought it was another ridiculous system to have the cashier in the supermarket behind perspex wearing a mask, but at the same time touching all your shopping as it went through the check out, touching your money and handing you your change - none of it made any sense!

We were told not to speak to neighours over the fence and not to let people use our toilets.

In the summer of 2020 Matt Hancock introduced the scheme, 'Eat Out to Help Out'. So we all went to the pub - should have worn a mask - Oooops!

You were supposed to walk into the pub in a mask, wear it at the bar, wear it to find a table and then take it off to eat and drink. Did anyone ever think that this 'covid' would not attack us when we were eating and drinking?

There was a QR code at each pub, restaurant, cafe door which you were asked to download - it would read your phone and identify you so that if anyone reported they had caught covid when eating or drinking at one of these places, they could contact you and tell you to self-isolate for 14 days.

This resulted in thousands and thousands of people staying home 'supposedly ill with covid' in self-isolation even though they were well.

And then came news of the vaccine that would save us all.

I knew straight away I wasn't going to have it and both my adult children felt the same. My daughter came under a lot of pressure in her workplace as a 'Carer' and I received letters from Somerset Council strongly advising me to have it.

The doctor's surgery consistently sent me messages and letters offering appointments to have it. I ignored them. At this point I no longer had any trust in anything the government said.

One of my elderly clients had it because of pressure from his family - he knew I wasn't having it and couldn't care less. The other family never asked. Common sense and my knowledge told me that a 'safe and effective' vaccine could not have been developed and adequately tested that quickly.

Also, I knew no-one who had covid and I knew no-one who knew anyone who had covid. In the entire 'pandemic' I knew of no-one who had covid except that one farmer, and I felt a little suspicious of that death.

At the time the vaccine talk was ramping up, advertised by celebrities, royals and prominent popular talk show hosts like Piers Morgan, I remember having weekly zoom meetings with my extended family and when I told them that I wasn't having it, they told me I was taking a massive risk and putting others at risk, that I was being irresponsible and that I shouldn't be able to work. They didn't mind speaking to me on zoom!

We were told repeatedly that the vaccine was 'safe and effective' via the media, and repetition makes a fact seem more true, regardless of whether it is or not. I would be interested to know how many doctors, nurses and regular people researched every ingredient of the vaccine before deciding to have it, or in the case of the medics, inject it into others including children. We now know the vaccine was not 'safe and effective' - there are many that are vaccine damaged and it didn't do what it said on the package which was that it would stop you getting covid and stop you passing it on.

I never considered travelling abroad as we were told we couldn't travel without having the vaccine. However, I know of many people, including family members, who had it specifically because they wanted to travel. How annoying for them when in fact we all found out that people were travelling without having had the vaccine!

We were told that there were no flights, although we then discovered that there had been daily flights around the world throughout Lockdown.

I was concerned for my granddaughter whose education was stopped, she couldn't take her GCSE's in the summer of 2020 and she was upset. Her work was evaluated and she was given GCSE grades, but she was very disappointed as she had wanted to be at school with her friends in the last months of her school life and take her exams. Instead they were all at home fit and well.

My grandson was a plumber. He was furloughed during Lockdown and thoroughly enjoyed it - he was paid 80% of his wages and had a great time with his friends. After Lockdown, getting back into his workplace he was immediately under pressure to have the vaccines and had two, to be able to work and travel. I was sorry for him as he also had felt under pressure from me and his mother not to have it, so he had them without telling us at first.

We were told that ethnic minorities were more susceptible. My granddaughter fell into this category - my daughter was worried. Schools were closed and my granddaughter was at home so my daughter gave up her work to be home and support her. Despite pressure, both decided not to have the jab and both are fit and well five years on.

Looking back I think the Lockdowns destroyed many people's confidence and created anxiety. Suicides increased, mainly young men - what a tragedy. The elderly weren't allowed to see their families and I think it shortened a lot of lives with them feeling unhappy and isolated. Lockdowns killed a lot of local businesses and I can't imagine what it did to young children, only seeing people in masks, not being allowed to socialise, and seeing their parents living in fear - the damage that was done!

Post-covid the financial damage to the country is in plain sight.

I am still working as a Carer and covid is never mentioned and I'm still happily walking dogs and riding horses, thoroughly enjoying living in rural Somerset.

The mainstream media's emphasis has shifted away from covid and is now focussed on the issues of climate change, taxing and restriciting farmers, immigration, welfare cuts, freedom of speech and turning their backs on the elderly and needy, but that's another story!

On the bright side, for me, and I think for a lot of people, we had time to reevaluate our lives and we learnt that we couldn't rely on the system. I learnt to trust my own judgement and intuition. With covid as the catalyst, so much is now being exposed and so many more people are questioning.

We are not just born to work, pay the bills and watch the TV each night telling us what to do, how to do it, what to eat, what to look like, what to drive, what to hate and who to hate.

Helen

Personally, in the post-covid years I would now never use pharmaceutical drugs unless absolutely essential. I now question everything that we're told by the government and the media. It confirmed my scepticism of the 'so-called experts' and made me realise how indoctrinated we are, how gullible and easily manipulated the majority can be when in a state of fear.

'Repeat a lie often enough and it becomes the truth.'

Simon

In 2020 when I first heard the word 'Covid' I was terrified. I had always thought life was good and something might happen to make it not so good, but I never expected a deadly virus!

At this time I lived on my own in a little flat in a quiet town in the UK, and so from enjoying the social side of my work and a great social life intermingled with visits to family, I was plunged into isolation within weeks as the first lockdown hit.

I was working for a company in London at the time and within weeks I found myself working from home. At first, although I missed my work buddies, I thought 3 weeks at home was a bit of a holiday, but as it got longer and longer with no sign of change and only terrifying news, it was a different story. I missed my work colleagues, friends and family and the Zoom calls didn't fill the gap. I became anxious as I didn't have anyone nearby and I felt very isolated. My girlfriend and I had decided not to lockdown together as she thought 3 weeks with her parents would be nice, but it wasn't 3 weeks and suddenly she was stuck on the other side of the country.

Every night I watched the news and seeing the numbers of Covid deaths rise, it seemed there was no end in sight. Looking back I was pretty much on my own from April until the end of June.

I did go out for walks 'on my own' as the weather was nice but I was always coming home alone to hear another barrage of statistics - it seemed neverending and there was never a word of hope.

I passed people out walking in masks which I found unnerving - they were alone and outside in the fresh air and I questioned the necessity of the mask wearing.

I shopped alone and found myself queuing to get into supermarkets. People shuffling around with masks on and eyes down - it really seemed like the end of the world had hit us! Children in pushchairs staring up at masked faces and without the usual chatter, everywhere felt soulless.

By the summer of 2020 the lockdown was lifted but I wasn't asked to return to my office and so continued working alone from home. The government produced a scheme to get us to eat out more - it was something like 'buy one get one free' in restaurants and cafés. Everyone was out and about and the eating places were full of people taking advantage of this government scheme, everyone was just pleased to be out again.

Most were still wearing masks. I found it comical that people would wear a mask until they were sitting down and then take the mask off to eat and drink - of course this was necessary, how could you eat and drink with a mask on, but it made no sense. As soon as people got up to go to the toilet they put the mask on and as I sat there I wondered to myself - 'do people really think that this virus will only attack them if they're walking around, but they're safe when they're sitting down eating' - it made little sense to me.

Actually the whole encouraging us to pack into cafés made no sense with this deadly virus still lingering, however, at this time I did what I was told and followed the rules. It was very nice to be out and about again.

The question going around and around in my head was "If there really is this deadly virus out there would anyone want to spend time in crowded indoor public spaces or were we all so stupid that we literally did what we were told.... one day stay at home and you can't visit your family, and the next day take a voucher and go into a crowded public space." I noticed that some cafes, pubs and restaurants did not open again - they did not survive that first lockdown.

I got through the autumn and then another lockdown, which meant I couldn't go home to my parents for Christmas. I remember this hit me hard! My girlfriend and I hadn't survived the year, not able to see each other we just drifted apart. Christmas alone was very sad.

Leading up to 2021, the news of a vaccine to save us from the virus was being talked about and by the start of the year it was all we heard of. To begin with I had thought, like millions of others no doubt, that it was fantastic that a vaccine had been produced so quickly to combat Covid, but the speed at which it had been produced and the constant promotion of it, like nothing before, started to niggle at me.

We were assured by the media in the form of newspapers and TV presenters, even royalty endorsed it - they told us it was 'safe and effective' - if we took it we would not get Covid or if we got it we would not get it so badly and we would not spread it. The guilt factor was enormous and hugely played upon. They were basically saying if we hadn't killed granny during Covid, if we didn't get the vaccine, we would surely kill her then, so one way or another we were a very bad person if we didn't.

TV presenter Piers Morgan, apart from endorcing how safe and effective it was, went on to say that those who did not get the vaccine should not be allowed access to the NHS for any treatment! Many others got on their podiums and said similar.

However, I had learnt during the last 15 months to start questioning what I was being told, as more and more months went by, so much didn't make sense and I didn't need to be a scientist to know this. I put my common sense hat on.

Did I really need it? I was young (in my twenties) and fit - I had been working out at the gym 2 or 3 times a week before they were all closed in lockdown. I played sport and had always had good health.

Over the months, as the vaccine headed towards my age group, I took the decision not to have it. Many of my family and friends were horrified that I wasn't going to have it and I was under a lot of pressure, but something in me shouted out that it was not necessary. My friends were planning a holiday but I was told I couldn't travel unless I had it, in fact many of my friends had it just so they could travel. Little did any of us know that everyone would soon be travelling regularly again - the threat of vaccine passports never came to anything!

I started to be excluded from social occasions and the TV continued to tell me consistently that I was a terrible person. I stood firm, I had looked at what was 'in it' and decided NO. I tried to persuade my parents and brother not to have it, with no luck.

My life had changed . It had really changed and people were judging me as never before. It wasn't nice, but there was no going back.

After the lockdowns, the isolation, that time alone which I'd never experienced before, followed by the refusal to have this vaccine, everything was different.

I look back and can't believe what we went through. Life has increasingly changed since that time. I look at the trail of destruction left by the lockdowns and it has undoubtedly left many lives destroyed. Although I never knew anyone who died from covid, indeed I never knew anyone who knew anyone who died from Covid, I now know many people, including people in my age group, who have been seriously ill after having the vaccine. I know of people who know people who have died after having it, but it seems no-one joins the dots, no-one talks openly about this. I am so glad I didn't have it. With all the information about the vaccines now I would be more terrified than I was of the virus if I had had it.

We hear of people, including young people with heart and blood problems constantly, and people with what they call turbo-cancer. We are told it's normal but it's not. I know it's not, I don't have to be a doctor to know it's not.

Since 2021 I have found many friends with similar views to mine and now have a whole new friendship group including a beautiful girlfriend. I also work for myself now which is a step I probably never would have taken before, as I was happy in my work before lockdown, although it was a bit mundane. I am more fulfilled working for myself, so lockdown served me well in that respect.

My life is very different than before and in most ways I would say life is much better. I learnt to be my own person and had to take some big decisions during the Covid years, and with all the information coming out now about the government parties back in 2020, when we weren't allowed to see each other, I think they knew all along that there was no need for masks and social distancing, otherwise they wouldn't have done it.

Looking back specifically at the lead up to Christmas 2020 when I was talking with my family about how we would spend Christmas, and then shortly after that, taking what we thought at the time was the right and responsible decision to cancel it, I now realise that at this same precise time Boris and his mates were planning a Christmas party (and that's just the one they were caught out over, for sure there were plenty more) and now it turns out that our current PM Keir Starmer was entertaining an actress at his home, allegedly for voice coaching lessons - whatever they were doing, they were breaking the very rules they made and we were obeying them.

When I think of us, the average person, following the rules and being kept away from our grandparents in care homes and our loved ones in hospital for months on end, while those that made the rules broke them, it makes my blood boil. How dare they. Will people ever forgive or trust them? They never gave us a moment of hope during the lockdowns, they only terrified us with numbers of deaths and we now find out that during that time, anyone who died, whether a car accident or whatever, was certified as death by Covid. No-one died of anything else during that time! Mmmmm - I don't think so.

Did Covid exist? I now think a new strain of flu existed, it was bad and a percentage of people suffered from it and some died. Was it a deadly virus worthy of shutting down the world?

No. We now find out that the average age of 'death by Covid' was 82.

Hardly a cause for what we went through.

PS - and I think we are on the brink of finding out much more and that will be for the next book!

JB

Be nice to yourself she said!
Easier said than done.
I mean there is an awful lot to contend with most of the time.
Like what could go wrong next?
Like should I or shouldn't I?
How much is that gonna cost?
What if it breaks and I can't fix it?
Is my memory going?
Why am I walking so fast but not keeping up?
Where is everybody?
What if they think I'm stupid?
What if I am stupid?

Why do I get everything wrong the first time
and probably the second time?
I've had enough of being on one long learning curve.
Where are my keys?
My wallet?
And bus pass. I am over 60.
Everything should be easier now but it's not.
I'm not sure how I got this far; I'm definitely not doing it again.
Certainly not without a hard hat and a high viz slip on thingy!
I'd murder a cup of tea. You know… builders tea… milk and sugar…
and tea leaves in a pot… not a bag
Thank you

Robyn

My partner and I have always discussed spiritual, mystical subjects together with the psychology of humanity, which led on to other subjects including government systems, controls and indoctrinations. People researching alternative news always tell you to follow the money, so that is what we did and it opened up the biggest story about the truth of humanity!

The information we came across was based on factual accounts first-hand from above top secret whistleblowers, many of which were military people. I set this scene to illustrate the things we learnt from 1995 onwards, such as the horrors of 9/11 being anything but that which was reported at the time. Now however, years later, most people do not believe the mainstream narrative.

We discovered from trusted people online that there was a nefarious agenda to reduce the world population and that we were being poisoned with toxins in every area of our lives, and most of us did not have a clue what was going on! These whistleblowers revealed that by the time the viruses started to come out, that would be the final act of the play.

Then came Covid-19. We had no jabs, didn't get tested, never wore masks, saw through the ridiculous nightly Boris appearances and the Monty Python script, mocking the people in plain sight.

My job as a Wedding photographer was halted abrupty as we were locked in our homes. We had to abandon our house building plans and instead decided to pay off our mortgage.

My partner lost his job. Neither of us could work. I found one way to earn some money by going out, staying 6 feet away from people with my telephoto lens, and taking pictures of families who would come to their garden gates with their long unkempt hair (no-one could have haircuts, remember!). I charged each family £10 cash for about 3 images and everyone wanted to join in. After all there was nothing else to do! We were all locked away.

When eventually I was allowed to restart my job there were restrictions for Weddings, first for up to 6 people, and then up 15 people, then 30. There were rules about wearing masks in the ceremony. I saw lots of people getting stressed, being unsure about what they could do. Most people followed the rules without question. Masks on, Masks off. Registrars arrived with helmet-type visors, a mask on inside the helmet, carrying a sterilised pen in a plastic bag and wearing blue gloves. If it wasn't so tragic it would've been funny, and there were a couple of times I could've laughed out loud, but just had to stifle it and walk away.

One Wedding, on New Year's Eve, seemed very sad. Everyone was made to wear a mask and from my perspective it just looked ridiculous. I was photographing a room full of masked people. You couldn't see their faces, even the bride's father had a mask on. After the Wedding was finished, the registrars went off to their next Wedding and the bride and groom were very upset about the masks. I asked them if they wanted to do it all again without the masks and they said yes. I had a word with the Wedding venue people and everyone agreed we would do it all again and that they could take off their masks. When I looked around, absolutely everybody had taken off their masks and when the bride and groom turned round to look at their guests, they all gave such a loud and long rousing cheer that I felt emotional. This was real. We needed to see each others faces. It provided a connection that was being cut off.

In another Wedding at a Devon beach resort they were only allowed to have 6 people.

After the ceremony we went to the beach for photos and because they didn't have lots of guests, I asked passers-by if they wanted to be in the picture. Some shuffled past, clearly terrified and others almost leapt into the picture, thanking me profusely as they waved goodbye.

I was left feeling how much people need to be together, not only with friends and family but also with our wider human family, whether they're aware of it, or not.

Moving on, 5 years later, my 'Wedding World' has returned to normal, not a mask in sight.

My greatest desire is for the collective human spirit to awaken and rise in radical change, so that our precious children can enjoy a glorious future.

There seems to be numerous narratives running in the media right now but the only thing I trust is my own instinct, my gut feeling, my 'take' on what feels true day to day, moment to moment, as we navigate through information overload and AI. It seems we are in a time of great change. Keeping my personal discernment and vibration high is my continual work.

Ben

In the Spring of 2020 I was travelling - I had been travelling for some months and had intended to continue, but with the persistent alarming news of Covid, I decided to head home and restart my travels when it was done.

I headed home to the UK and found it to be quite crazy from my arrival at the airport; if I hadn't been unduly worried before, I certainly became super-worried as soon as I set foot in the UK. I had first heard of Covid some weeks before when I was travelling through the area in and around Las Vegas, and no-one was really taking much notice at all, l but in the UK things got serious. Finding people masked, heads down and no communication was surreal.

I headed home and got on with it. Apparently the masks and social distancing were put in place 'just to be extra careful' and things would be assessed and re-assessed as the days went by and more information became available - 3 weeks to flatten the curve seemed perfectly acceptable as no-one really knew what we were dealing with.

Days turned into weeks, and weeks into months with no apparent hope in sight. Summer came and went and I made the decision to postpone returning to travelling until I felt a bit more certain of the way things were going; there was talk of a 2nd lockdown. I picked up some temporary work and settled down to a rather strange life in England.

By the autumn there were two conversations going on. The first was of the impending 2nd lockdown and the second of a vaccine being ready to help us out of this worldwide pandemic by the New Year.

The thought of a 2nd lockdown was gloomy, especially as winter approached - things seemed as though they couldn't get much worse. I made plans for Christmas, but always had a little voice in my head saying 'remember this may not happen' and so I was mentally prepared when the Christmas plans were cancelled and the hope of the vaccine was a least a light on the horizon.

I had made up my mind towards the end of 2020 that if our government was telling us to do something for our own good, backed by the science, then that's what I would do.

The New Year of 2021 came and I waited for my age group to be called by the NHS. When the time came I was relieved and I met many other people that day equallly relieved, at last we were being offered something to stop this virus spreading.

I had a 2nd vaccine, a booster, a year later, but after that there was just too much conflicting information for me to feel assured that the vaccines were 'safe and effective' and 'would stop the spread'. I saw no real debate about the pros and cons of the vaccines.

With the information available now, I am glad I stopped after having 2 and wish I hadn't had any.

The TV presenters and others who had fought hard in promoting the vaccine, indeed had ridiculed and vilified the few who had come onto their shows giving another opinion, went quiet, and now 4 years on we see some of them publicly backing down and giving rather pathetic explanations of how they got it wrong and 'maybe' they were a bit fierce in their promotion.

I can only imagine they have a hard time sleeping at night when they consider how many millions were listening to them and trusting them at the time as if they knew what they were talking about.

With all the information we have now, those who made their final decision based on what the likes of our TV presenters and the odd rock star said, as I did, must be feeling a bit misled to say the least, as I do.

As if those people ever had any real knowledge to be able to promote a health initiative.

Where are you now Dr Hilary Jones? I listened to you as did millions of others, because you were a 'doctor' - I thought you knew what you were talking about. Let's have an explanation of how you got it wrong, or even an apology. I listened to you. What exactly are you saying now Piers Morgan, having said back then that people who chose not to have the vaccine shouldn't have access to the NHS? I hear you making lots of excuses now but I haven't heard an apology.

Are either of you visiting those who now have lost their health after having the vaccine? Are you visiting the families of those who have died? Tragically this includes many young people. Unfortunately the government who sternly told the people of their country 'to have the vaccines, or else...' followed by the list of things they couldn't do... are not listening to the vaccine injured now.

When I look back over the past years, I think I did the best I could - I did what I was asked to do back in 2020 when none of us really knew what was going on and it was all terrifying. I believed the government, but I don't believe what they say any more as I don't think they did the best they could at the time - there was a lack of basic common sense in what they were asking us all to do. Going on from there, there are now many instances we know of when they didn't follow their own rules, and that's shocking and distressing to most people. If they didn't follow their own rules we have to ask "Why?" Did they know that this was not a deadly virus - common sense tells me they did, otherwise they would have been the first to follow their own rules.

Looking back at the harm that was done to so many as a result of the lockdowns, I don't think there was ever a case for shutting down the world.

All the small businesses that were lost, it's a terrible thing. There should be some sort of compensation, a scheme now to help people build up their small businesses, and their lives, again. When you think of the millions being spent in other directions which the public haven't voted on or given their support to, why hasn't any attention been paid to those who lost their livelihoods?

I do know people who died in 2020 - they didn't all die of Covid whatever their death certificate said. We are now told that the average age of death in 2020 was 82 - I rest my case. I know of more people whose health has been affected since having the vaccines; previously healthy younger people who are now disabled and unable to work, and I know of people who know people of all age groups who have died or become seriously ill after vaccines.

I live now with my very own common sense hat on and think very carefully about anything and everything that will affect my life. I have lost the trust I once had in those that make rules for the rest of us.

Politics across the world has gone crazy. In the UK we have a Prime Minister who takes away from the pensioners of his country and pledges millions to other countries to fund wars - no vote on this, although he supposedly represents his people.

Other 'interesting to say the least' things have happened in various countries, and the big one was the US election in November (2024) when Donald Trump was re-elected. His inauguration was on 20th January 2025 and since then the bad press has continued. There are many who still rant and rave against him, while I watch and listen in the background wondering why they haven't stopped ranting and taken a pause to see if he does infact carry out some or any of his promises.

Personally, I would like the top guy of my country to say that he was on the side of the people, the people's wishes and the people's children's dreams, that he will not start new wars and will end existing wars, that he will tackle immigration, fraud and criminal activity and put his country first, and, last but by no means least, that he will take on the pharmaceutical industry with the help of the UK equivalent of Robert Kennedy and 'Make the UK healthy again'. I would actually like that.

Donald Trump has said all of that to the American people, let's wait and see what he actually does... having never been interested in politics.

I now watch closely and am cautiously optimistic.

By the way, I never returned to travelling - perhaps one day when the world makes more sense I will feel the desire to pack my bags and take off for a while!

Until then I'm enjoying my front row ticket to 'The Greatest Show On Earth' and I can't even begin to imagine where we will be one year from now, but if there's another book I'd like to carry on recording my point of view into 2026 and beyond!

PS.
Recently, I saw this on the UK government website:
'As of 19th March 2020, COVID-19 is no longer considered to be an HCID (Highly Contagious Infectious Disease) in the UK'
This was just days before we went into the first lockdown, so it leaves me asking the final question... "What was it all about?"

I am the Love.
I am the Light.
I am the Truth.
I am.

www.blossomgoodchild.com

The coding within these words spark off
an Energy that gives you
Comfort, Strength, Hope, Trust, Security …
You name it …
This Mantra will satisfy your 'need' every single time.
Let it Be Of You.
For it is you.
You are nothing other than this!
With Love, Blossom

Janet Jackson Tyler-Lummer

DO SOMETHING !!!!!!!!!!!!!

Now that life is back to a new normal, basically I am playing catch up with my finances. I am getting bills paid in great anticipation to be able to save again.

Being that I am in the entertainment business, I had years of making no money, which put me in a hole that I now have to dig myself out of.

However, I know God, and he knows everyone, so I will, through his grace and mercy, get through this and be very grateful and at peace. Faith is a great spirit and I am happy I have it and understand it.

My thoughts at the end of summer 2024...
Our world is getting ready to change in a big way and I am looking forward to the change that I am expecting. It is time for a Woman to become President of the United States, and I believe in my soul it is going to happen this November 2024.

Kamala Harris is the right Woman and her pick for Vice President, Tim Walz seems to be the right person for her running mate. It feels so right and I believe they are REALLY for the PEOPLE. I look forward to voting this year.

I went home to America that autumn to see my brother. He had been in cancer treatment during that year and he was basically getting to the end of it; I had a few weeks free to go and be with him in person. Thank God for internet, because I had been able to talk to him on video every day, which kept me calm because I could see how he was feeling, but there is nothing like really being there and I was looking forward to our time together for real.

My brother is so very different from me; I like to talk a lot and he does not, so when I first started calling him every day, at one point he asked, "Why are you calling me everyday?!!!" I said "I am just checking on you." Then I stopped calling for a few days, then I called again and he said "Why did you not call?!!!" 'Can't win for losing' as my Mother used to say. Then I realized he had gotten used to me calling and realized he liked it, LOL. But of course he would never say it. We are 4 years apart. He is 74 and I am 70.

My trip was so fulfilling. My brother was doing very well. He was very happy to see me and we got many things done that he needed, and I was at great peace about his condition because I could see he was wanting to be active and he is moving around like he is not sick, and that was so wonderful to witness. He even BBQ'd. He also bought another truck, so that showed me he expected to live. My brother is blessed and highly favoured and all our prayers are being answered by God.

During my trip that autumn of 2024, I went to the Democratic Party Office in Santa Barbara, and the office was CLOSED on a Friday at 11.30am!!! I was very surprised and disappointed. That is the middle of the day and it should have been open. So I could not volunteer and I could not donate.

I had written online to ask to volunteer for a registration drive at SBCC (Santa Barbara City College), but no one wrote me back to let me know if it was possible or not. I only had 14 days in the city so that is why I contacted them as soon as I came into town.

When I returned home to Spain I wrote to them, and I was also on a streaming conversation with Democrats Abroad, and I let them know what happened, in hopes they would contact the Santa Barbara office as well and see what is going on with the communications not being thorough. It was so important that EVERYONE VOTES. It was IMPERATIVE.

While I was there, the Democratic convention was in progress and I heard a speech from Michelle Obama that struck a cord with me. She said at the end of her speech "DO SOMETHING!!!!"

I never will forget I read somewhere years ago "If you can complain about it, then you can do something about it" and that is so right!!!! I realized I was that kind of a person and I had been doing that most of my life, but never thought about it, because it was so natural for me to react in this way.

When I returned back to Spain (Alicante) there was a town hall meeting being telecasted from America which was hosted by Oprah Winfrey and Kamala Harris. There was a mother in the audience who was there with her daughter. Her daughter had been a victim of a school shooting and the mother was distraught by what her daughter had been through, and how children go to school to learn, but they also have on their minds "Am I going to be killed today?"

Just writing that now brings tears and sadness to my soul. I just cannot believe this is happening to children on a regular basis in America and STILL there have been no regulations on gun control in regards to assault rifles, which are the guns that are mostly used for the school shootings.

When I saw this mother I just broke down sobbing. I thought "I have to DO SOMETHING."

When the mother was speaking she said "It is time to fight for our children", and I knew what she was saying was correct and then I remembered the organization:

MADD (Mothers Against Drunk Driving)
www.madd.org/our-history/

After sooo many people had been killed by drunk drivers and nothing was really being done, mothers came together and made the greatest change ever for their children. I believe the force that these mothers used in creating legislation to stop the madness, is exactly what the mothers now have to do to save their children killed in schools today.

MADD is in their 44th year and are STILL making changes for the better, and I personally do not know one person who drives drunk anymore. Those mothers are the ones that made 'designated drivers' a household phrase. Created in 1920 in Scandinavia.

Over the years, MADD has been instrumental in getting drunk driving laws passed and the legal acceptable blood alcohol level reduced. By 1982, more stringent DUI (Driving Under the Influence) laws were introduced in 35 states and passed by 24 states. A year later, 129 new DUI laws had passed, and the snowball effect continued (Google 2024).

I wrote to MADD and suggested they get in touch with these mothers that have lost their children to gun violence in schools, in hopes they can give them the organizational skills and connections they have to fight for their children. Perhaps they can start another department that deals with gun violence.

I hope I will hear from them. On the website it says we will be in touch with you. So I will stay diligent and contact them until I hear from them.

I will let you all know what happens!!!!

I wrote my story at the end of summer 2024 and it is now a year later, and a lot has happened in this last year. All I will say for now is, as you know from my story, things didn't work out as I had wished over the election in the U.S. so now we watch and see what will happen next...

We, that are still here after the pandemic have a reason to live, so let's find out what it is and DO SOMETHING.

'Always in Spirit'
Janet

Bob Dibden of the New Forest, England

Navigating an Orwellian Dystopia

I was brought up in the 1980's. In my teenage years during the Reagon/Chernenko period when the nuclear arms race had intensified between the United States and the Soviet Union, as depicted in Frankie Goes to Hollywood's 1984 single and music video 'Two Tribes'.

Films such as 'Threads' and 'When the Wind Blows' vividly portrayed the bombing and the ensuing nuclear fallout. Luckily, I suppose that as I was young it did not seem real, and I was more concerned with my own life than that of the wider world.

During the 2010's I had come to gratefully realise how lucky I was never to have been involved in a war that directly affected us.

But that was about to change. This war was not against another country, but against its own people, and across the world. This, I believed, was World War 3. Johann Wolfgang von Goethe is often quoted as saying, 'The best slave is the one who thinks he is free'. In a similar vein, one might argue that the most effective way to wage a world war, for whatever the reason, is to ensure the people being attacked remain unaware they are the target. This provides the aggressor with a distinct advantage.

It was February 2020 and there were stories in the news about a virus sweeping the world. It felt just like the swine flu story when a few years earlier, fear about a 'fictitious' flu was spreading in the media around the world. Shortly after, a swine flu vaccine was launched.
Over 30 people were harmed from the vaccine, so the vaccine was withdrawn due to the very serious harms it caused to people's physical health. The narrative about the swine flu and the vaccines then disappeared from the media. This was how I thought the coronavirus story would play out. I did not think it would develop into the dystopian nightmare it would become.

I had been questioning everything since around 2010. I had watched a documentary film called 'Zeitgeist' which covered the topics of religion, 911, and the financial system. Each well-analysed topic also was littered with countless red flags that would suggest, that at the very least the subject was dubious or questionable, or at the very worst, a complete lie. It made me think that just because I had been taught something as a kid, or an adult, doesn't mean it is true. It had activated my bullshit detector or intuition, and to then question everything.

When the UK announced on 23rd March 2020 that it would be going into lockdown, it felt like a weird and troubling time. During the first lockdown I had two choices; to either read more about health, or to eat myself to oblivion to cope with how instinctively wrong it all felt. I fortunately chose the former. I then read two fascinating books in April; one called 'What Really Makes You Ill' by Dawn Lester and David Parker, the other 'Vaccines: A Reappraisal' by Richard Moskowitz. Both contained a huge amount of logical analysis.

I remember in January of 2020 I'd asked someone I knew who worked for GP practices how effective the flu vaccine was at preventing flu. She said they did not have the data, and no patients ever asked the question. I could not understand why people would not ask this basic question before deciding to roll up their sleeve and have the injection. They just assumed it would help because that is what they had been 'told'.

Having read 'What Really Makes You Ill' with its compelling evidence and critique, I came to believe that colds, flus and viruses do not exist. 'Dis-ease' is something the body is in a state of, and not something you 'catch' from someone else. I was happy for anyone to cough in my face who had any cold, flu or so-called coronavirus symptoms. I was not in any fear about any virus, but in fear of what draconian measures we were under, and possibly were to come.

In April 2020 the government launched the first Nightingale hospitals. These temporary emergency hospitals were set up to treat the government's predicted number of patients suffering from covid-19, as the coronavirus started to be called.

At the time the government asked any retired or ex-doctors and nurses to volunteer to help in these hospitals. The father of a guy I knew who lived in Exeter volunteered. He arrived at the one at

Moor Lane which was set up to cover the whole south west of England. He stated that when he arrived, there were only five patients present. Why would the country lock down its population when a regional hospital only had 5 patients? Something was not right. The hospitals were not overrun, that was for sure.

I also spoke to a lady who ran a couple of care homes. She told me that one of the elderly people in one of her homes had been taken to hospital. The person had pneumonia. During this early period of 'the nonsense' as I call it, the hospital said she had to take the old person back into the home. A few days later the person died. A doctor phoned her up and said she had to put cause of death down as covid-19. She challenged the doctor, and she said that the person had been previously diagnosed with pneumonia. The doctor forcefully said to her she must put covid-19 on the death certificate. Clearly fraud was at play to exaggerate the perceived threat.

When the government made face coverings mandatory on 24th July 2020, I did not want to comply. It felt deeply wrong and there was no evidence they worked. I was not going to wear a mask. This was bullshit. The government had previously said masks were ineffective but now had changed their mind.

How was I going to handle this? I had read that you could go to the government website and print off an 'exemption' badge. This badge said you were exempt from wearing a mask. I kept it on me when going out in case I really needed to show it to get in somewhere. I rarely needed to show it as often when quizzed about not wearing a mask, I would just say "I am exempt", and that would be sufficient.

I had also found online a 5-page document about my legal rights to not wear a mask. It stated that according to government guidance, you could claim exemption without showing a printed badge.

If someone challenged you, under the Equalities Act of 2010, they had no right to ask about your medical conditions. Asking for such information would be breaking the law, causing stress, and violating GDPR (General Data Protection Regulation) rules.

I faced this challenge at Tesco. When the doorman asked about my medical condition, I told him he had no right to know and that asking me was causing stress. I also mentioned that both he and Tesco could be liable for up to £9,000 in damages. Then, I walked in. I was extremely anxious that first time, but I was not going to bow down to this ridiculous tyrannical rule. A couple of times I was harassed by other customers in Tesco. I rarely saw people in there not wearing a mask.

I remember, shortly after the end of 'mandatory' mask wearing, one checkout lady said to me "You're the guy that doesn't wear masks aren't you?" I was easy to spot of course.

What I could not spot of course, was other people's reactions to me not wearing a mask because their mask would hide their anger and distain.

In September I ordered a newly released book called 'Corona False Alarm?' by Dr. Karina Reiss and Dr. Sucharit Bhakdi. It was packed with information that clearly demonstrated how the statistics shared by the government, especially those from Prof. Neil Ferguson of Imperial College London, regarding potential sickness and death, were grossly exaggerated and false.

I remember the headlines in newspapers back in the spring that said, "Half a million dead, 8 million hospitalized." It sounded at the time like over exaggerated scare tactics. The same scare tactics were use on 28th May when the government launched the 'Track and Trace' app which was a special whole page article/sheet covering every single daily newspaper.

According to the book 'Corona False Alarm?' it does state that this is not the first time Neil Ferguson had over exaggerated potential risks. He had predicted 136,000 deaths due to mad cow disease (BSE), 200 million deaths to avian flu and 65,000 deaths during the swine flu – in all cases there were just a few hundred. When they said "Trust the science" that should have been a red flag for everyone.

On 5th November 2020, a second 4-week lockdown was imposed. I had heard about a protest march taking place that day, so I decided to drive to London. People were not meant to be driving more than 5 miles from their home. The drive to London was very quiet. The roads were dead. Leicester Square was empty. Dead London.

I walked to Trafalgar Square where the protest was due to start. There were some people around, but dozens and dozens of police were everywhere. It was a climate of fear. Police were stopping people and asking them for their ID and where they were from (to verify that they were within 5 miles of their home). It felt like this was East Germany in the early 1980's when people were being asked for their papers. There was a time and a place for a protest, but that evening did not feel like it was one of them. I decided to drive home. Next day I found out that a lot of arrests had been made.

Christmas 2020 is a day that will forever be etched in my memory. It was the only time I was to ever wear a mask. I would usually spend Christmas day at my mum and stepfather's home. They had decided it was not safe to spend the whole time having a Christmas lunch, but instead to spend an hour having a cup of tea. My mum insisted I wear a mask or could not go. I agreed very reluctantly to wear one to not upset my mum with my absence. We could not see each other's faces obviously. It felt very wrong that hour.

On 6th January 2021, a third lockdown was imposed. I did not want to be here. I was in a dystopian world. I had felt that from March 2020, until probably January 2022. I relished going to sleep to escape this madness only to wake up back in this dystopian reality again. As a fan of science fiction, I could not watch any dystopian TV series, because I needed something lighter to escape the darkness I was experiencing. Mask wearing, social distancing, 'Track & Trace', 'bubbles', the 'Rule of 6' and the regional 'Tier' system were all tyrannical fear-based nonsense. There was also talk of vaccines being rushed out, which seemed to follow the same playbook as the Swine flu.

It eerily mirrored the dark comedy Channel Four TV series 'Utopia', where a fake news story about a virus was used by the government and media to push a vaccine on the population, making them more sterile and reducing the global population. Interesting.

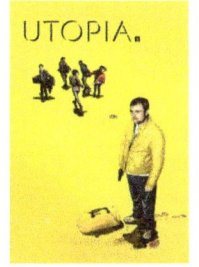

In 2021 I had read and seen images about a 'camp' that had been set up in Australia to keep those that had refused the jab, and 3 massive camps were planned for the UK. These were worrying times.

I did not understand why people were interested in taking vaccines. We were told that covid-19 was just like a 'bad flu'. I had never had a flu vaccine and not had flu in over 20 years. So, if I had not had flu, nor was I concerned by flu, would I be concerned by the so called covid-19? Of course not. Even the government leaflet issued in the early days of the first vaccine rollout, telling people to take the vaccine, suggested only those over 60 or those who had health vulnerabilities should take it. I thought to myself, the vulnerable are the last people that should take an experimental medical procedure. I was not in the so-called 'at risk' category; I explained this to my family, yet they wanted to queue up for it.

My close family, including my sister and her family, as well as both sets of my parents, showed little interest in my opinions. My dad said just 'take the jab'. I said taking an experimental medical procedure was breaking the Nuremburg code. I'd left a copy of the book 'Corona False Alarm?' with my sister, but again, she was not interested. I begged her not to allow her children (my niece and nephew) not to have the vaccine. Again, I was ignored. I remember a few of them gathering at a social event, all having gotten their first shot, and comparing their 'side effects'. I couldn't help but feel despair listening to them.

During those first 2 years I was not allowed inside the house of my mum and stepfather (except for Christmas day 2020). We could meet in their garden 2 metres apart. My mum would not allow me to hug her for those 2 years. In June of 2021 it was my 50th birthday. My mum and stepfather had offered to take me out for lunch to celebrate my special birthday. My mum offered to pick me up if I wore a mask in the car. I replied saying I am not wearing a ridiculous mask but would meet them at the restaurant.

During those 16 months they had barely left the house; just occasionally to walk up the road to the park and back. When they arrived near the restaurant I met them near the car park. They both had big masks on and looked like a couple of scared mice. It was horrible to see. Fortunately, as the meal went on, they stopped wearing their masks and we had a nice time.

Between lunch and dessert my mum needed to pop out to the car park to extend the parking time for their car, so I walked with her whilst my stepfather remained at the restaurant. She confessed to me that my stepfather had had a mini stroke a few days earlier. I was aware that he had taken the second jab around 10 days earlier. I told my mum it would have been the vaccine that caused it, but she shouted "No!". She didn't want to hear it. Curiously enough my mum has hearing issues. My stepfather about a year or so later did 'manage' to say that his aphasia symptoms started around then.

I had four close male friends at the time who all took, I think, at least two of the experimental vaccine jabs. One so they could go on holiday, and two of them to keep their marriages. I had explained the madness of it all, but they ignored my pleas. That said, whenever we got together, we would hug upon arrival, although the wives would not hug me for a couple of years. Although we had different opinions on the subject, they did not judge me, which was very much appreciated.

In September 2020 the 'Rule of 6' came out. This is where you could go to a restaurant (as long as it was outside only) but only have a maximum of 6 people. I went with my friends. They all wore masks in the taxi, and all wore them when leaving the table and going inside the restaurant to use the toilet. It was ridiculous.

Dating was a different experience. I went on a few dates during the lockdowns. I remember one date on 14th February 2021; the weather forecast was cold, wet and windy. Very few places were allowed to open. I did not want to meet in a supermarket as it did not sound great for a first date.

I did think a launderette might be the answer if the weather really was terrible. Fortunately, I knew that if we went for a walk and the weather turned bad, we could still meet in a covered archway at a nearby castle. The weather turned out quite pleasant in the end, although the lady serving outside drinks really was not happy serving me without a mask.

One way to cope with the insanity in 2020 and 2021 was to go out on my bike in the New Forest, sometimes with one of my very good friends. Few people had ventured on to the forest, especially when the government said we could not go out for more than an hour's exercise per day, which of course I ignored like every other restriction. I really got to appreciate the New Forest more than I ever had before. It felt 'normal' being there, unlike the programmed phrase 'new normal', which seemed to have been used very quickly and a lot at the start of 'the nonsense'.

In August of 2021 I met up with my cousin and cousin-in-law round their house one evening, as I had not seen them for a couple of years. To my surprise they had not been vaccinated. At last, I had some members of my family who saw the insanity in it all. I was on such a high for the rest of the evening. Why was everyone else so compliant to these ridiculous lies?

I felt very isolated in my views. One voice of sanity during this period was James Delingpole. I listened to his podcast. It felt like just him and I knew it was all a fraud. The voice of reason.

I went to a live event of his in October 2021. Someone at the event told me about something called 'A Stand In The Park'. This is where like-minded people would meet in towns and cities across the world at 10am on a Sunday morning; people concerned about 'where it was all going'.

I found there was one near me at Barton-on-Sea on the clifftop, and one on the hill at Boltons Bench in Lyndhurst. I turned up on a cold windy Sunday morning and twelve complete strangers gave me big hugs. It was very emotional. I smiled like a Cheshire Cat for that hour I was there. I had found my tribe. I was no longer alone.

In 2021 and 2022, I went to a number of the big London marches, including the one in early 2022 when the nurses threw their uniforms into Downing Street; a very powerful day. I did wonder if I might have to give up my work as a mortgage adviser. Given care workers were fired if they had not had a vaccine and NHS workers were heading in the same direction, I thought that my network might say to me that if there was a potential that I might see a client on a face-to-face basis, that I would have to take the jab to 'to keep clients safe'.

I also offered to help my cousin and cousin-in-law financially should she lose her teaching job for not taking the jab. Fortunately, my cousin and I were not forced to leave our jobs as mandates around the UK started to end during 2022.

Whilst this was a dark period in history, it did make me appreciate nature a whole lot more and I've met some of the nicest people during this period. Sometimes when you experience darkness you appreciate and have more gratitude for the light.

"I am grateful for so many things and for the connections I have made both within myself, with others, with nature and with all that is."

I am inspired by the wonderful Veda Austin in her work with water, in that water has both memory and access to collective consciousness.

I felt it really important to connect with the waters both on a physical and energetic level, as everything is energy.

Being of and on the New Forest, I intuitively felt that the good people of the New Forest should have access to good water from the ground.

My quest is to find springs and wells across the New Forest. It's going well and I now collect my drinking water from a spring on the forest.

To find out more check out the facebook group:
'New Forest Wells & Springs'

Much love,
Bob x

JB

I wish I could remember
Could remember all those places I've been to
Could remember all those people I leaned on
Could remember all the phases I've been through
All the people I once knew
Who are forgotten
In the dream that is today
In a place that's far away
In the time called yesterday
Gone behind
I dare not look
Where's it gone?
I'll take you there and we'll share
What's left of the time that's passed
We'll walk in times of nostalgic memories
Where only what's sweet lives on
That's the way it should be
Only the good survived
Who needs what's not needed
Not you not I
Memory suppresses what it doesn't like
Thankfully we can smile at what's passed
It's all long gone
It didn't last
I'll venture on with a mind to yesterday
But with a foot in today

Over and out.

Belinda

I was terrified when Covid arrived in March 2020 - I had seen the news of the virus in China and people dropping down dead on the street. It never crossed my mind that it would spread across the world, but in a very short period of time it did.

Thankfully the UK and other countries went into a lockdown to protect us all and we were adivsed to wear masks and distance ourselves from other people; this made sense to me and it made me mad to see some people not abiding by the rules.

I watched the news each evening and spent the rest of time hoping for better news the next day, but it was endless gloom and despair; each night the reports of the number of deaths was horrifying and I remained very frightened of this deadly virus. I felt I had to trust those putting the statistics together although it was pretty scary. I called it my 'Daily Dose of Doom'.

Belinda

I worked from home and went out as little as I could, just for essentials, and although I didn't have a garden I had a nice balcony which had sunshine for part of the day, so during that first lockdown when it was so sunny I spent a lot of time on my balcony in the sun. I heard people walking by, still quite a lot of people wandering around, out and about - I had no desire to join them. The roads and the skies were quiet and I liked that. The birdsong and the sunshine was lovely.

I lived on my own with my cat, Florence, and so it was easy to follow the rules and do everything my way. Florence came in and out as she pleased so no change for her! When I walked out to shop for food I wore my mask - I had bought a lot of them when the whole thing started so I had plenty. I kept away from other people and was a bit scared when other people came too close. For example, outside the supermarket they had painted where we should stand on the ground so it was easy to be at the right distance, but lots of people didn't stand where they should.

In a local town they painted arrows on the street so that it was clear we would walk up one side of the street and walk down on the other side - I thought this was quite sensible to help us keep at a distance.

I do realise that things weren't as easy for other people. I had friends who thought the whole thing made no sense at all, and although we survived the first year talking about everything else except what was actually going on, and our extremely different opinions, when the vaccines were introduced we had nothing left to talk about. We gradually stopped talking and we haven't started talking again since then.

I had a friend whose Mum was in hospital and with all the rules, although my friend was prepared to go along with everything, it made things complicated and made her very sad. Another friend's Dad was in a care home and from one day to the next he was unable to visit him during that first lockdown, and by the time he could visit him his father had gone downhill and was very disorientated seeing his family visit him in masks and visors; he didn't really understand what was going on and he died in the autumn of 2020.

Despite the fact that I agreed with the lockdown, I do recognise that many of our old people died unhappy, in some cases frightened, and alone and all of that is a terrible thought.

By the time the vaccines came along I was relieved and continued to have boosters and more vaccines over the years. Until now my health is OK, although I am aware of more and more news coming out now about many people who have had adverse reactions. I do find a lot of the vaccine discussions very worrying but I did what I thought was the right thing to do at the time for me and for those around me.

Looking back over the past 5 years I see that life has changed, my way of life has changed and I spend quite a lot of time wondering what will happen next and wishing things would go back to the way they were pre-2020, but I know they won't.

One thing I miss a lot is travelling. Living alone I used to travel a lot, booking organised holidays, visiting really wonderful and often exotic places, I met some lovely people, some of whom I am still in touch with. I miss that a lot and try not to think about it as I have no wish to travel now. Perhaps one day.

Belinda

Over this last winter in the UK the relatively new Labour government has neglected the pensioners and made some bad decisions, they call them tough decisions but in my opinion they are bad because they are not benefiting the people at all, and what they seem to have forgotten is that they are there to represent their people. I have begun to take anything they ever say with a huge pinch of salt, often accompanied by a huge sigh of despair. There are bad situations across the country, particularly in the big cities and things we used to hear of going on in far away places seem to be going on on our doorstep now. I don't know what will happen next.

The governments seem to go from bad to worse, and not just in the UK, and I think what we have now is more than a disaster, I hope things will at least get a bit better in my lifetime but I really don't know! 'I take one day at a time.'

Bob Hellyer

It's coming up to six years now since the start of the 'pandemic' and I don't think the world will ever be the same again! It was an eye-opener which forced some people to see beyond the visible - others, they didn't really know what was going on.

From the start I knew there was something wrong. It seemed there was just a complete knee-jerk overreaction to something which seemed no different to a flu outbreak, but the longer it went on, the more I was convinced that there was some huge manipulation of the people going on across the whole world, and I couldn't understand why people couldn't see what I saw!

The years that followed exposed the huge amount of corruption in the world as a whole, and the massive damage that powerful corporations were and are causing.

All in the name of 'profits' and 'philanthropy' amongst other things.

In the UK we are witnessing many generational farmers being forced out of their livelihoods, the only lives they have ever known. Prices are being driven so low that they can't survive. They are forced into mono-crop culture because that brings in more yield, but within this shift, any goodness in the soil is being destroyed by the fertilizers and insecticides. This process causes the topsoil to be washed away leaving the fields desertified. Not only do we lose our fields, but it is a major contribution to weather patterns, and sadly this is the guideline of the corporate-ruled governments in action.

'They' are trying to stop farming - plain and simple. Instead of wholesome food being grown, the poor farmers have to grow seed oil crops that produce toxic oils after processing, and grain feed for animals rather than grass which is their real food... The list goes on! We are forced to eat processed foods, which are harmful to us, because 'real' food is hard to get and expensive.

The above is only an example of how we are being deceived! We could go into Pharmaceuticals, Banks, Insurance companies, Energy companies, Arms dealers... Politics and all it encompasses!

All this enlightenment came about by the 'Lockdown' perpetrators showing their hand six years ago! That was a big mistake, letting us see, because now they are scared of what we have seen and once you see, you can't 'unsee'.

It may well get worse before it gets better, but we will keep on fighting for Truth and Free Speech, which is the latest attack on our freedom.

Personally, I don't listen, watch, nor read 'The News' and am blissfully happy with that! Too much fear-mongering and untrustworthy opinions! I listen to the Radio Caroline album station - no news and only adverts for music and second-hand cats.

However, that incident six years ago was a bookmark in many people's lives and for the majority of people, life will never be the same again. Others are going about their daily lives hoping it will get better and go back to the way it was, completely unaware of what's really going on.

What happened in 2020 changed the life of my family completely; we chose to leave Spain, a place we loved, and in turn start a completely new chapter. I moved back to the UK in 2022 and in the last three years I have met a few good like-minded friends and am enjoying the life I have made for myself here, but I do miss the Spanish weather!

After I retired I had started producing digital art and that kept me going through the 'Lockdown' years, some of my art features throughout the 'Memories' books. I carried on in earnest once resettled in 'Avalon' - the lovely county of Somerset.

In fact, one could say I've become possessed - ha ha! I just love it. Sometimes I get up in the morning, turn on the computer and the next thing I know it's 4pm, and I haven't even made a cup of tea - but it's so satisfying!

I do the occasional artwork commission and design bespoke greetings cards. I exhibit in a gallery now and then, but luckily I don't have to make a living from it. Pressure free is my desire, but if anything sells, it's a nice compliment!

My son Joe bought me a stone-tumbling/polishing machine for my birthday last year, which I love. I've now bought a second one and they are running constantly. So much so that I've had to buy replacement motors as they burn out after 6-8 months.

It's amazing what some stones actually look like after polishing. We have a lot of aggregate around our town, and you may well spot me examining the stones by the edge of a path, looking and occasionally finding little treasures.

I have also spent many hours learning from tutorials on wire-wrapping stones. Another hobby that I really enjoy. Unfortunately we don't live near a beach, but if anyone is going to one of the beautiful Devon or Dorset beaches, I ask them to bring back any interesting stones, and if they find one they particularly like, I will polish and wrap it for them. Guess what people get for their birthdays?

Life goes on, and more and more gets uncovered as regards the legal(?) underworld. I suppose that's the way it has always been and it will never change if we just let it keep happening!

Don't think you can't make a difference, because you can! Even the smallest little things from each of us can make a difference, and lots of small things become something BIG!

Emma

I live in New Zealand and when, in September 2021, I had a call from my family saying my father in the UK was dying, I thought I couldn't possibly go to him because of the difficulty at that time with returning to New Zealand, especially getting a place in *MIQ. Then my cousin rang me and said, "No, you've got to go because you will never forgive yourself if you don't." "But how will we get back to New Zealand?" I asked. "MIQ has special places for people who have had a bereavement" she told me. So I decided I would go.

For those of you not familiar with MIQ - it was a quarantine system which had been in place since April 2020. Under the system, people entering New Zealand were required to isolate at an MIQ facility for 14 days. Compulsory Managed Isolation.

My partner and I were running a hospitality business at the time, and were also busy organising building consents and a ton of other things. It was complicated, however, my son offered to run the business for us while we were away so we started to prepare for the trip. There was a lot to sort out before going, and one of those things was arranging a PCR test. We had to have a negative PCR test result within 48 hours of our flight departure. I'd never had a PCR test and didn't know what was involved; just organising that was a minefield. The airline didn't help, they insisted we had to have the test before booking a flight, and the people doing the test insisted the flight had to be booked first... Eventually the airline let me book a ticket without having a test.

We arranged a flight for early on the following Saturday, September 21st which meant we had to be tested on Thursday 19th. It was a long four and a half hour journey by car from home to the airport, and I had a great deal on my mind - the business, the tests and all the paperwork that we needed to travel - 'fit to fly' paperwork. It was incredibly stressful!

Without any internet on the trip to the airport there was nothing more I could do. I felt stressed, helpless, and fearful about everything; about covid, PCRs and vaccinations. So at one point on the journey I just decided to be in the present moment, and as I was sinking into that moment I noticed how stunningly beautiful the mountains and scenery were all around me.

All of a sudden I felt expanded and a part of everything. In that moment all the stress and fear fell away. I heard a voice in my head say, 'You are always OK - no matter what happens you will always be OK - even if you get vaccinated you will be fine.'

I knew this was true and that I was always going to be OK.

We got to Christchurch and booked a hotel for a couple of days so we could do the test, wait for the results, sort out our 'fit to fly' paperwork and register with the MIQ website to apply for places upon our return. During that time I rang the MIQ helpline to find out if I could get a special place if I needed it. The helpline operator I spoke to knew less about everything than I did, and he was really upset because of the people who couldn't get back into the country, people who had a dying family member, or who were expecting babies, and how horrendous it was. I ended up supporting him!

Sadly, at 01:00 am on the Saturday morning, before flying, my sister rang to tell me that my wonderful father had died. I was so grateful for my earlier experience because I knew that we were always OK.

In the UK at that time there weren't the same restrictions as in New Zealand. However, before we left New Zealand we were required to get another PCR test kit posted to us in the UK, then on the second day after arrival in the UK we were required to do the test and post the results back; this meant we could go wherever we wanted for two days, meet as many people as we liked and then post the test to whomever. If it turned out to be positive I don't know what would have happened; I suppose they thought that we would have to find somewhere to isolate for a while, but it struck me as quite nutty because obviously travellers are going to visit lots of people. So what was the point of another test?

We departed on the Saturday morning and after long tiring flights, we arrived in the UK on the Sunday afternoon.

That Sunday night, Monday morning (NZ) MIQ digitally opened its doors so we could queue to get a place, Until then, because of the threat of covid, MIQ had been closed for a month, so now, with the doors re-opening, there were loads of people, who had not been able to get back home, vying for a place. After an hour, I was 100 in the queue, my partner was 6000!

Arriving in England, I was quite fearful, I didn't know how we'd get around, or what the conditions would be like. Should we catch a train? What would that be like with covid around?

My father's funeral was small, not because of covid, but because that's what my stepmother wanted. He was buried on his property with only family in attendance. It was lovely and afterwards we decided spontaneously to have a Wake for him.

Over one hundred people came; it was a joyful occasion, no-one wore masks and everyone was happy to be there. There were a couple of people who said they would be coming, but didn't, one of them was a very old friend who I'd known as a child, and afterwards I found out that she didn't come because my nephew had tested positive for covid, and my friend's son had been in a car with him. Knowing about his positive test and his determination to attend the Wake, she had decided not to attend, but unfortunately without telling me. At the Wake my nephew had given me a massive cuddle, no mention of the positive test and this was two or three days before we were due to leave. When I found out he'd tested positive I was quite angry because he could have jeopardised our flights back to New Zealand. I had thought 'What if he'd passed it on and I got a positive test?' I could just imagine the headlines in the national papers back in NZ 'Covid in MIQ!'

In the UK people weren't wearing masks anymore or isolating for two weeks, and there wasn't any MIQ. Meanwhile, in New Zealand everything was ramping up and going nuts. Every day the case numbers were announced on TV, and the system of constantly changing alert levels was keeping everyone uptight and anxious. Quite honestly, looking at what people were talking about back home, I thought that if we hadn't had the business in New Zealand I wouldn't have returned because it was so horrible and toxic and fearful, and that was before the vaccine passes for accessing various services were introduced later that year.

When it was time to fly back to New Zealand, we had to have another negative test result to get on a plane; another time-consuming hurdle getting it done and getting the timing right!

'Welcome to the Bonkers Hotel'! On arriving back in New Zealand our masks were taken from us at the airport and we had to put on N95 masks. We were put on a bus and taken to the MIQ hotel for our two week incarceration. There were soldiers everywhere, which was quite bizarre.

At the check-in I asked the guy, "You haven't got the honeymoon suite, have you?" When we got to our room we found only one paper bag containing a meal and a drink. I realised he had indeed given us a different room and that they hadn't supplied the second meal to our new room. It wasn't quite the honeymoon suite, but it had a very tiny balcony and a door that opened onto it which gave us fresh air, which we were very grateful for! There was also a locked door that led to the room next door.

We had literally been in our room for about twenty minutes when someone knocked on the door to do a PCR test. They shoved the swab up my nose and made it bleed, which continued for three days. I pulled myself back and said, "I'm not doing that!" And they said, "We're the best in the world at doing these PCR tests." 'That's strange' I thought, 'because I've had a couple now and neither of them were like that!' About an hour later I got a phone call. "So you're a refuser, are you?" "What?" I said. "You're a refuser of the tests, are you?" they said. "I'm not refusing to do the test, I'm just refusing to be abused by that person" I answered.

Within forty minutes of wearing the N95 mask the back of my throat and my chest were hurting. I told them, "I can't wear those masks." They said, "Well, you have to wear them if you want to go outside." "But it's causing me physical pain" I said. "Well you're going to have to find another one. You can get something delivered to your room."

In the end I couldn't actually get an alternative. So they said I could wear my own mask with one of the N95s on top. They said these masks are the best in the world and there's a brand new box of them in our room. I looked at the box and the label said 'Made in Wuhan'. How bizarre, I thought... wasn't it a Wuhan fish market where the virus had mysteriously originated? Or was it in the nearby virology lab? What sort of crazy, mad world had we descended into?

Our hotel room was nice with a big TV - interestingly the first image, when you turned it on, was MIQ information. It also displayed the times for us to go outside for exercise which changed daily. The hotel was virtually empty when we arrived but over the first week it gradually filled up. As more and more people came in, our exercise time got shorter and shorter and the times each day never made sense, there was no pattern to them. I'd think to myself - OK, so if we're going out at 10am this morning it's likely that tomorrow we'll go out at 11 or 12, but it was never like that - it was completely random!

After nearly two weeks of our stay at the 'Bonkers Hotel' our only outside exercise time was at 5am! At lunchtime they would bring us a newspaper which was supposed to tell us all about what's going on in MIQ. Well, this newspaper looked to me as though it was written for eight-year-olds. On the first day it had a cartoon picture of a very simple cupcake with a square grid next to it; the instructions said: 'Can you draw this cupcake?' Lots of the pictures were cartoons of other cakes. I thought this was all very strange, so I rang them and asked, "Have you given us the right newspaper? This one seems to be for children." They said, "No, we just thought it was fun, because it's International Cake Day." They promised the next ones would be better but they weren't. They were all designed for children with the occasional item about someone smoking outside on a balcony, or upstairs, and reminding us that smoking was not allowed in the hotel.

The 'bubble' thing was interesting; we had to stay out of other people's space and keep at least two metres apart from everyone except for the members of our 'bubble'. In the morning we would get a telephone call to say our breakfast was outside. We would have to wait and then open the door with our masks on and grab our breakfast from outside the door and then quickly close it again. It was the same for all meals.

One day we were outside having a walk in the designated area when we started talking to another couple and they said, "Oh, you're in the room next door to us. We know when you get breakfast because your phone rings and then we know our breakfast is coming an hour later. We're not allowed to come out of the door at the same time as you to get breakfast, yet we're all allowed to go out at the same time for our walk!" They also told us, "We love it when you open your door to the balcony, because then we get some fresh air." Nobody else could open their

windows. I thought to myself, 'We're supposed to be in managed isolation and yet the air travels through our room into theirs'?

While they kept us apart and confined to our social 'bubbles', it also happened that all the occupants of our floor congregated outside the lift when we were allowed to go outside. And yet inside the lift we were supposed to maintain our 'bubbles'. In the beginning that was fine; there weren't many people around, but suddenly, every time the lift appeared there were people already in it. We discovered that the floor above us was getting the lift before us. So we worked out that if we pressed the lift to go up instead of down, it would open for us before it got to them.

Every time we went downstairs the army were there, and they'd walk around with us. There was one army officer who walked closely to the couple in the room next door. He would walk around them as if he knew them. He would practically touch them but later say things like, "Oi, oi, you've all got to be two metres apart." Totally bonkers!

We also met a single guy from the UK in MIQ who had only come back to New Zealand to do up a house that he owned, and then fly back again. He too thought that the whole two weeks in MIQ was ridiculous. Occasionally they posted that we could go for a walk only to cancel it. There were many odd things like that. It felt like they were trying to confuse us… it was bizarre.

We used a lot of imagination... to fill the days I would say to my partner every morning, "Today we're going on a trip," or "we're going along the canal," or "we're going for a walk in the mountains." We also watched many movies and read a lot. I'm just so grateful that we got that room with the door that opened, and that we had a fantastic view. We overlooked a beautiful park, with mountains in the distance. Others weren't so fortunate.

'Home again'
When we got back home and to our business, the pub, I found that everybody was really scared of me. So for another two weeks we didn't go into the business because people were so freaked out. After we did go back in, we held an event which was attended by a lady who I knew and liked, but who looked very fearful. I asked her, "Are you okay?" She said, "I'm alright, I've had my vaccines, but it's my children. I'm so scared for my children!" Coincidentally, my niece had just rung me on Messenger and said her two-year-old had covid. She had posted a video of her daughter dancing around with a toy I'd given her that she loved. I showed it to that lady and said, "There, look at this video, she's got covid and look, she's absolutely fine."

People were scared. We had other customers coming in saying things like, "Ugh! Christmas! Half my family wanna come but they're not vaccinated, so we're not letting them come." We'd say, "But you come here." And they said, "Well, that's different."

As we know, the vaccine was an experiment. We thought, OK it's an experiment and no-one really knows what's true and what isn't true. Let's just hold back a little bit and see what happens. My son was also allergic to vaccines and had once nearly died from one, so it was never an option for him.

In late November 2021, the government brought in the mandates which meant the business couldn't operate at all. We didn't know what to do at first, but thought that we could open for private functions which we started doing once a week. The police would show up demanding to know who was holding the function and wanted that person to identify all the people in the room so that they could prove it was genuinely a private function. A policeman also started driving into our car park when we weren't open, taking photos of parked cars. I complained but they denied he was taking photos.

On Facebook lots of people were trying to shut us down, and boasted about how amazing they were when they succeeded. We had a lot of people mentally and verbally attacking us. We were even afraid that the locals would turn up with pitchforks because they knew we hadn't taken the shot. The irony was that the media and government were saying the vaccine won't stop you getting covid and won't stop you spreading it, though it may stop you dying. We knew by then the chances of dying from covid were similar to dying from the flu, so none of these measures made sense to us.

It cost us thousands and thousands of dollars trying to keep the business open in some limited way, and when the mandates were dropped, people didn't come back. We were known as those people who had not shut their business. In hindsight, we wish we'd never opened the business in the first place. That would have saved us so much time, stress, and money.

There is a 'silver lining'...
Curiously, I heard recently that Jacinda Arden (Prime Minister during covid times) had been up north looking for somewhere to live - she was in a café with the estate agent when she literally got chased out by angry, upset people. Whilst I really understand that a lot of people hate her and want revenge... I mean, obviously I would love to see justice and I would love to see people acknowledge what really happened and to have the balance restored... however, I feel grateful because if we hadn't gone through the hard times, we wouldn't know now how strong we are.

We grew strong. We found something inside of ourselves that feels so solid. We see now that what happened was about fear. We just don't feel that scared anymore. We know that we are more resilient and resourceful than we ever could have imagined, and with that resilience and resourcefulness, it's OK to be joyful, to be happy.

Right here, in this present moment, there's nothing bad happening.

Conor & Lurdes

Our Lockdown Times

My name is Lurdes Nagore, and my husband is Conor Hannah. We are a married couple living on the Mediterranean coast of Spain, on the outskirts of the City of Valencia; we moved to this area in 2011.

We want to share our experiences during the Covid lockdown with you in these simple words.

I worked as a veterinarian at a small animal practice in Valencia, and Conor ran a business and a charity for homeless people at that time.

We first started hearing news about the virus in January 2020. The situation unfolding in China was shocking and looked very unstable. In February, the media began reporting a few cases arriving in Europe, and it was frightening to follow the rapid spread of the virus.

At that time, I knew the virus would eventually reach us so I decided to order face masks online because I anticipated that if the virus arrived quickly, people would panic, making it difficult to obtain them later.

On March the 14th of 2020, the Spanish government announced the lockdown. I remember arriving at my practice wearing a face mask three days before, and my colleagues looked at me with surprise. Days later, on a Friday, we were advised to stay indoors, not to leave our homes and not share the same air with anybody.

During that week, my eldest daughter who was 10 years old at that time, stayed home because she had a very high temperature that lasted for four days and the doctors couldn't determine the cause. Conor and I suspected she probably had COVID.

When the country declared a state of alarm and the lockdown began, it was an interesting period for all of us because we were forced to stay indoors.

In March and April 2020 when the virus was very aggressive, people were very stressed as they saw many people dying. We didn't know who would be mildly affected and who would die or develop severe pneumonia; it seemed random.

Conor and I considered ourselves fortunate because we live in a country house with fresh air and a garden to enjoy. We felt sorry for many people who had to stay in small apartments; it must have been much harder for them during that time.

Every day, we had the opportunity to go into our backyard and access the forest, and we could take our dog, Lila, for a walk.

This was important as it was only permitted to leave the house for dog walking or grocery shopping once a day. It was concerning because there were many police patrolling the forest as well.

Every day, I would go to the forest once for a walk, and I always took either one of my daughters aged 10 and 6 years old, or my son aged 9 years old, so they could also have a refreshing nature walk. We will always be grateful for that option!

Conor's parents were visiting when the lockdown started, consequently, they had to stay with us, as they were unable to return to their own home. With us, our three children and Conor's parents, there were seven of us in the house; we had to stay positive and organized.

We used a lot of imagination and established a structured daily routine; our household routine was full of activities. First thing in the morning was breakfast, followed by fitness and a shower. The children had some online school activities and played games - lego, ball, hide and seek in the garden and catch with the dog were the favourites - then it was lunchtime, and after lunch we allowed the children some screen time.

During the first weeks the children enjoyed the peace of not having to rush to activities or school; it was a very tranquil time and they were comfortable with their online school, but as the weeks went by they missed seeing their friends and they missed their routine. They kept up with their online school work but there was not enough, not the same amount of work as at school, but they coped well because of our outdoor space.

They returned to school in the September of 2020 and had to wear masks all the time, in the classroom and in the playground.

In the afternoon, we would walk Lila, have video calls with friends and play more games. We really enjoyed cooking, especially the baking; we all enjoyed baking together and cupcakes were the favourite!!! Our cooking skills improved significantly!

We had plenty of activities to try and keep everyone's minds occupied. We avoided sharing the news with the children, as we felt it might be too overwhelming for young ones under ten years old.

Life at home was quite peaceful, and the children experienced that time with a lot of bravery and peace. We were very fortunate that no-one in our household got sick with the virus at its peak.

My work was very interesting. I would work during the morning and come back home in the early afternoon. The police gave a special pass to me to go to work as animal medicine was considered an essential service.

At work, we had to wear a lot of protection, and unfortunately by mid-March masks ran out. I remember having to reuse them after a day's work and putting them in the oven to disinfect them. It took nearly two weeks before masks became readily available again, but then we had them for a long time.

I remember being very careful with masks and surgical gloves, which were also needed for surgery. At the peak of the crisis, we had communication from the state that they urgently needed more oxygen concentrators, so they recalled some of them from the veterinary practice.

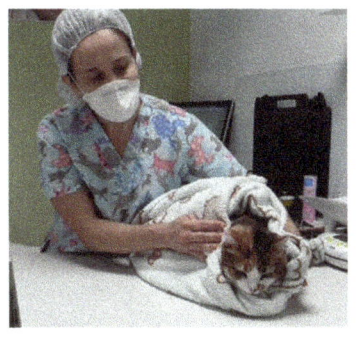

People were very nervous, and at work, we had to take the pet at the entrance of the clinic from it's owner, and two of us would take it into the consult room and examine it without the client present. We worked in teams of two nurses and a vet to avoid having too many people mixing, which reduced the number of people in the clinic. Most clients understood but some got angry.

We remember the COVID times of 2020 as a period that truly made us reflect on the breadth and depth of our humanity. It was a valuable time for families to bond with one another in peace, and it's important to recall the positive aspects that emerged during that difficult time when humanity was at risk.

While it was undoubtedly painful to witness so much suffering and the loss of so many lives, it was also a precious time to dedicate to strengthening our relationships, spending quality time together without the usual daily rush.

Conor had a very important job for the city because the homeless people living in shelters - March 2020 - were sadly unable to access water from fountains or get leftovers from people walking in the street, nor could they get cash from begging as there were no people around. Conor obtained a special pass from the police, and, after that first hard week, he quickly began bringing them food and water.

They had large water containers that were cleaned daily and filled with fresh drinking water so the homeless could wash their clothes, have a shower, and access all the necessities a human being deserves.

Later, the city provided the homeless with places to sleep in football pitches and large sports centers, where they could access water and food through ONGs (Fundacion Ayuda Una Familia) and the city hall.

Conor's ONG was also fortunate to receive donations from large industrial companies that supplied food for restaurants. As the restaurants were all closed, there was plenty of excess food available. Conor was very busy with his work and the charity.

As I returned from work in the early afternoon, he would go to his work all evening, usually returning around eleven at night. There was always plenty to do! Grandma and Grandpa were great company for the children throughout this time.

March marks the beginning of Spring and the March of 2020 was no different... with longer daylight hours and the blossoming of nature, our garden was beautiful and filled with peace. We were fortunate to have a peaceful home with sufficient resources to be comfortable, despite the situation, and at the same time, we could use our professional skills to help others during the terrible lockdown caused by Covid-19.

I felt deeply grateful to be able to offer assistance during that period of hardship. Helping each other allows you to add a positive element to adversity, makes you feel useful, and lifts your self-esteem.

Many people experienced psychological difficulties during and after the lockdown, being confined indoors and isolated forced us all to confront ourselves.

The arrival of the vaccine was a challenging time, as we knew it was very new and potential side effects were a concern. We were particularly worried about giving it to our children and how it might affect their development.

In the summer of 2021, a few months after everyone got the vaccine, we were allowed to get more social. That time truly tested our strength, even though being at home presented a low-risk environment. Life at home was very enjoyable as we were lucky to have good supplies of food and plenty of space which reduced the stress.

Looking back... thankfully, most of the time, everything went well, and we managed to stay positive. After the 98 days of lockdown in Spain, we were able to leave home, and the summer had arrived. Gradually things started to come back. We made an effort to stay informed without being overwhelmed by excessive negative news, and we focused on maintaining stability and peace at home during those difficult global times.

I am so grateful as well that the virus was not strong in children, that was a gift for humanity.

These are the most important memories from the lockdown that we wanted to share with you, hoping to convey that balance and peace are possible even in challenging times.

Daygan

In the Spring of 2020 I could feel there was 'something in the air…' I had lived and worked in Glastonbury for 25+ years and seen many changes, but had not expected the huge changes that hit us with the first Lockdown!

After my Dad passed away in 2019, I suggested to my Mum to come down to Glastonbury so I could take care of her. This was just before the first Lockdown. Perfect timing.

During the first couple of weeks I was still cautious, I didn't know what to think - the masks and the social distancing, but after 2 weeks I started thinking 'this is nonsense'.

My Mum, in her eighties, has various health conditions; in Lockdown she was in a lot of pain and decided to have a shoulder operation. I took her into hospital wearing an 'exempt lanyard' but I still got looks for not wearing a mask. Mum wore a mask under her nose.

She had to have various tests, and during her appointment with the specialist she saw an injection, amongst other things, on a metal tray. Luckily, she's sharp and asked what it was; the specialist said "We've noticed you haven't had the covid injection." She told him that was because she didn't want it. She didn't have the covid jab.

She had her operation, but unfortunately it didn't really work and they wanted to keep her in hospital. I saw her health deteriorating fast, her legs were swelling up, there wasn't the care to look after her. I worked really hard to get her out, I had to prove I could look after her at home - eventually I got her home. Her leg swelling went down, she just needed care. There were stories that the hospital was full, but it wasn't full - it was quiet, not many people there, not what was being reported.

Music has been a major part of my life from an early age, my passion. I had found a mandolin when I was about 8 years old; I taught myself to play and have been a musician and an artist ever since.

Music changed my life, and because of the music I was interested in, celtic medieval style, it brought me to Glastonbury decades ago. I became part of a band called 'Dragonsfly' and we've been playing together for over 25 years. My other band currently playing is 'Maythorne'.

We were playing gigs nationally and internationally, but when Lockdown came, the gigs stopped.

Luckily for me, living in Glastonbury, I would go up the Tor with my mandolin and play, and I continued connecting with people through the music, as human connection is crucially important.

To be in nature - the music - the stillness - that really saved me, and I recognised it as a Gift. I wrote many tunes in the 'Apple Orchard' in Glastonbury, at the foot of the Tor - the whole landscape there inspires me and I wasn't going to be stopped from being up there - it's my life.

In Lockdown, on a positive note, I liked the fact that there were no planes; I could cycle down the back of the Tor, and Chilkwell Street on the main road, on my bike, no-handed, in the sunshine, hearing the birds singing - a beautiful aspect of Lockdown! It was like a dream! For me and the many others who gravitated to the Tor, we didn't feel isolated, it kept a sense of community.

There were people about, but anyone hanging around would get moved on. The police even came up the Tor a few times, but they couldn't stop us from being there - we were in different parts of the Tor, outside in the fresh air, playing music, getting inspired.

The town was different, some businesses shut down completely, but other things kept alive. Most shops closed. I remember Speakers coming to Glastonbury and meeting in the Market Square. I and others played music in the Market Square; I have been boycotted by some because of my stance for freedom. I guess it was part of the plan to divide and conquer, create separation and confusion, whist keeping us distracted with nonsense.

I felt incredibly lucky that I had all my interests here, my motorbike, working on my garden, my ceramics and my radios. All the things I've been interested in since a very young boy.

Every night in Lockdown, the TV would give doom and gloom, numbers of deaths and never a word of hope. A dark Energy. It's crazy what went on and what's still going on.

In 2021 the vaccine arrived, the biggest advertising campaign I've ever seen. I didn't like the further division this created, and even now some people don't speak to me because I made the choice of not being vaccinated. It makes my heart bleed as I've got no problem if somebody did or did not want the vaccine, it's their body, their choice, but I chose not to have it as I consider it to be 'experimental gene therapy', and only a vaccine in name. My choice should be equally supported.

It's interesting for me now to see there are a lot of people retracting what they said, saying things like "You weren't being forced into having the vaccine and there was a choice." But the way it was pushed in the media it seemed like there was no choice. Jobs were threatened and we were told we couldn't travel if we didn't have it. I know people who had the vaccine because of their jobs or to travel, they didn't want it and now regret it.

Now - 6 years on - many doctors are speaking out against the 'vaccine' publicly and being heard. Thousands spoke out back in 2020 but were ridiculed, censored and not heard.

The companies who manufactured the 'vaccines' have said they're taking them off the market for various reasons, but at the same time they're still coming to the door, still promoting them, still saying they're OK for the elderly, for pregnant women and for the kids. I feel like this is a crime.

Bill Gates with his 'honorary doctorate' hasn't studied to be a doctor, and in my opinion, the tech-vaccine link is a dangerous one, though a very profitable one. Since the roll-out of the vaccines we've never seen so many heart attacks, blood clots, strokes and cancers. We have seen vaccine-injured and deaths in all age groups.

I've heard about certain detoxes to clear the body, frequency energy clinics and bio-frequency generators to interfere with the tech. For those who regret having the jab, this is better than burying your head in the sand. I believe there were a certain amount of placebo injections.

In my opinion the past years have been a throwback to the 1930s. I think it is wartime - distractions through the TV to take our minds off what's actually going on. The plan by the few to overtake the world and become slaves to them and their wealth - nothing to do with us 'thriving' - all to do with control. In Glastonbury we're lucky because there are many people with diverse ways of thinking.

When I look back to when my Mum was in hospital in 2020, I can't believe they tried to sneak a covid jab into her. At that time and since, I have received loads of texts to remind me that she hasn't had it, and the amount of times they've knocked at my door, 3 of them at a time, going door to door with the vaccine! However, I would also like to say that over the past years we have had the local NHS doctors out to see my Mum at home and they've been great.

There's something going on... there is a War - it reminds me of a book I read - 'Silent weapons for Quiet Wars' by Charlotte Graham. A War on our Air, Water, Food, Money, Weather, Freedom of Speech. Poisoning and Pollution. Vaccines and narratives not for our wellbeing. The people in power haven't got our best interests at heart, it's all to do with money and power and it's not supporting human life. Distractions - look over here while we slip through another bill over there.

Chemtrails, aluminium in the air - some pilots are now speaking out. Trees getting ill and there aren't as many insects and birds. Nothing is done to support nature, only attacking it and therefore attacking us. 5G and talk of 6G - it's a massive leap of technology - microwave tech links with tech which is in the experimental vaccine.

More freedoms being taken away, anything that doesn't go along with the narrative is being shut down and censored, People getting labelled 'domestic terrorists' for speaking their Truth, even people being imprisoned, creating fear for people to speak out.

I use cash when I can as this is our freedom. It's so sad how going cashless would affect the poorest people.

Cameras everywhere, on roads, motorways, traffic lights, in supermarkets watching exactly where you're driving and what you're buying. Against our freedom.

After living through the last 6 years I think the most important thing is our Health. I know people who come together to grow their own food, a wise idea for one and all.

Fields which once grew food now have solar panels, wild flowers, anything but food! If this continues we will lose our natural food and will be forced to eat plastic manufactured food. I believe we're not going to let that happen as more and more of us become aware of it.

Unity and Community is important, Lockdown taught us that; we need each other and we need to look out for each other, be kind, stop hurting each other, stop all the things that cause division, which is all man-made bullshit. The earth is hurting, the creatures are hurting, we are hurting - something is very wrong. We need to talk about it.

Ultimately I think it's about Connection and Celebration, positive thinking, focusing on our creativity and what brings happiness. We're super-powerful as sovereign beings, combining together and celebrating - super powerful. This is our Strength. We are infinite beings in a Universe of infinite possibilties.

Glastonbury attracts Dark and Light. It's full of musicians, artists and healers, but we get extremes here because it's magnetised. The Tor amplifies everything. We, the Light Workers, know about this. We can manifest what we want and I believe we have a choice and we will be given what we focus on, which is why I focus on my Music and speaking my Truth. We need to return to love, to be our authentic self, look at our shadow side to help the Healing, to return to Love.

A lot of conspiracy theories are not conspiracies any more, they're actually fact.

Once a percentage of people wake up and share information with others, we will see the whole consciousness shift. I think the waking up process has accelerated, there are many more people questioning everything.

HOPE - I do feel hopeful as we are raising the vibration. I search for the Truth. Detox your system from metals and plastics, get out in nature and give yourself time and space away from technology. As more and more people do the same, we will go forward into the future we want to live in.

Keep focusing on what makes you happy!

Hayley

My life has changed completely since the beginning of 2020 when the world locked down. The circumstances in Lockdown led me to meeting Armand, and to the story I am going to share with you in this book...

In the September of 2023, I was heading off on holiday to Latvia with Armand to meet his family for the first time. I was excited and nervous - would they like me and would we be able to communicate? They did and we could! We had a lovely time!

Visiting Latvia was very special; it was the first time Armand had been back to his homeland for 10 years and within a few days of being there, we received some amazing news!

We had a great week sightseeing with his parents, and the amazing news we received was that I was pregnant. We were surprised and happy and decided to keep it a secret for 3 months, which was very hard as we were so excited!

Seeing our little baby at our 12 week scan was amazing and made it all feel more real, and just before Christmas we found out that we were having a little girl, which we had both secretly hoped for. We could finally choose a name and Armand created the most beautiful nursery - we had everything we needed.

We attended hypnobirthing sessions together and felt prepared for having the home water birth that I wanted. However when baby arrived 8 weeks early, the consultant decided I should have a caesarean section. This was my worst nightmare.

Baby 'Freya' was born at Taunton, Musgrove hospital at 02.05am on 12th March 2024. We had been sent to Taunton from Yeovil as it was better equipped to deal with premature babies. Armand was by my side at her birth, and we were very nervous and excited to meet our daughter two months earlier than expected!

They brought Freya over to us and put her on my chest all wrapped up and with a hat on. We could only see her little face but she looked perfect. Then they took Freya to the NICU (Neonatal Intensive Care Unit), it felt terrible being separated from her, but Armand checked on her and five hours later, when I got the feeling back in my legs, he pushed me in a wheelchair to see her. I was still in a lot of pain.

At 07.30am I held Freya properly for the first time, so tiny and small, and making little noises.

She was here already - it felt surreal and amazing that I was now a mummy, a bit daunting at how small she was and what our journey would be with her arriving so early.

My mum and brother came to meet Freya but no-one could hold her as she needed rest, and had lots of wires attached to her.

Due to concerns about Freya, we were transferred to St Michael's hospital in Bristol, specialised and better equipped for her needs.

St Michael's were concerned about Freya's jerky movements; there were lots of wires, tubes, needles and machines monitoring her and giving her various drugs which was a lot to process and made it difficult for us to be able to hold her. One drug was Midazolam which we knew from Covid times was often given as an end-of-life drug so that worried us a lot, but they said it was to stop her having seizures.

It would be a week before Armand held Freya and before I would hold her again.

When Armand held Freya, three nurses helped to move her with all the wires and her ventilator that was strapped to her little face.

Our days were spent by Freya's incubator, touching her through the little doors on it, praying to receive good news and for her to get better.

It was a very emotional and worrying time, with us just willing Freya to get well enough and strong enough to go home with us.

Many of our friends and others, plus online communities were sending healing and doing all they could to help get Freya better.

A few days after arriving at St Michael's in Bristol, we found out Freya had contracted the Herpes Simplex Virus in the womb and it was in her blood, and had caused encephalitis in her brain. It's extremely rare and there were more questions than answers.

Receiving this news was a devastating blow and the outcome looked as bleak and bad as it could possibly be. Armand was back at work and my Mum came to to be with me.

We were given very comfortable free accommodation at 'Cots For Tots', opposite St Michael's and there we waited the longest four days of our lives for news from the specialists.

My Mum was with me to hear the news, with Armand connected to us by phone. We were told how severe Freya's predicted health would be if she survived. Receiving this news was our worst nightmare - absolutely devastating. Nothing can prepare you for it and you just hope to God that Freya's diagnosis was wrong, that they were wrong and that she's going to be fine.

Freya looked perfect and healthy, despite being eight weeks premature. How could we even think that she wouldn't live or contemplate life without her? We were faced with the prospect of saying 'goodbye'. Would our relationship survive?

We had made the extremely heart-wrenching difficult decision to take Freya off her ventilator due to her very complex and life-changing condition, and we would see how she coped. We weren't sure if she would survive, and if so, for how long.

Family came to meet and potentially say goodbye to Freya.

Freya had had some of the wires and needles removed, plus some drugs stopped or changed so we could see how she coped. The nurses said that Freya knew I was her Mummy as her stats always became more stable when I was with her.

On the 23rd March, I was feeding Freya an hour before the ventilator was due to be taken off, when suddenly she coughed her ventilator out of position.

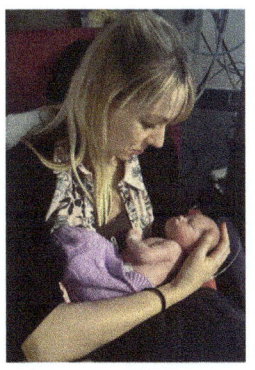

Freya kept on breathing and the minutes turned to hours, the hours turned into a few days and we were so happy and tried to feel positive that maybe the diagnosis wasn't quite right.

Four days after the ventilator came off, on the 27th March, an ambulance arrived to transfer us back to Taunton hospital. Although I felt sad to leave St Michael's and the amazing staff, I was excited to be closer to home and easier for family to visit.

However, returning to Taunton wasn't great. The staff weren't as friendly and efficient. Our room was basic and opposite the labour ward so I could hear women giving birth day and night, which was very distressing. Very different to the lovely facilities and staff in Bristol.

Freya seemed to be doing well and if she continued to do well, we were looking at taking her home in around 4 weeks.

Armand and I discussed the medication Freya was being given 'Keppra' (side-effects included seizures, jerky movements, and other severe conditions) and 'Phenobarbital'(side-effect breathing difficulties).

They reduced the drugs, but when another seizure occurred, they upped the dose, without speaking to us. We were worried but the consultant didn't agree with us. Things started to get worse.

I kept notes of possible side effects which I thought could be causing the seizures. I didn't feel listened to; they believed in the drugs and their protocol. I hated seeing so many drugs going into her little body.

Freya was being given 'Phenobarbital' when her seizures were hard to control and stop, the machine bleeped, she was going a grey-blue colour. They quickly put a small oxygen mask over her face, and administered oxygen. This was scary, worrying and horrible to witness.

Eventually Freya was breathing better, and I couldn't help but wonder if it was the 'Phenobarbital' that caused her airways to close.

On Wednesday 10th April the day was much like the others. At around 5.30pm she had a seizure which I recorded. At 11.30pm I left Freya to get ready for bed. One of the nurses came for me and said Freya was having a seizure, and they couldn't stop it. She'd already been given one dose of 'Phenobarbital' and they were preparing another dose as per the protocol. I was already worried about how much she was being given, especially as she had stopped breathing the day before.

I rushed to NICU following the nurse and got to Freya's incubator to find three nurses around her, and my heart sank. Somehow, I stayed calm.

They had called the consultant back into work and I knew it was because they thought Freya was going to die. I called Armand.

Armand arrived not long after the consultant. She spoke with us and said we needed to decide what we want to do, what was best for Freya, more drugs and the ventilator back on, or to let her slip away.

The consultants had told us how severely affected her quality of life would be, and would it even be a life, would it be fair to her, would she want to live a life like that? This was the worst thing to hear.

Selfishly I wanted to put her back on the ventilator and give her more drugs, I didn't want to let her go, to give up on her, to not give her a chance and to be thinking I'd be planning her funeral and not her birthday parties.

I thought 'why had she chosen to live after her ventilator came off, why hadn't she passed then, why had the seizures started up again?'

On Thursday 12th of April at 02.15am Freya passed away in our arms aged thirty-one days old.

Our hearts were broken.

We spent some hours with Freya in a special room, dressed her and cuddled her. The second hardest decision for me was deciding when I would put Freya down, knowing it would be the last time I would hold her and see her. I kept delaying putting her down, crying and kissing her, not wanting to say goodbye forever.

Our dreams of being a Mummy and Daddy cruelly taken away from us, our daughter gone, the nursery all decorated and ready with a wardrobe of clothes, nappies, and wipes all there waiting for a baby that would never come home with us.

Calling family to give them the news was so hard, but they all rallied round and Armand's colleagues helped him too.

We found a beautiful place to bury Freya, with gorgeous views, meadows and orchards with just small placards next to a tree to mark graves. We thought this would be perfect. The celebrant read out a letter we had written to Freya and my brother spoke, which meant a lot to us.

The flowers were all lilacs and purples as that was Freya's colour, it represented the crown chakra and area of her body that was affected. We also asked everyone to wear these colours too. We played songs by 'Bliss' from the album 'A Hundred Thousand Angels' during the funeral and at her graveside, as these were songs I played to Freya a lot when I was pregnant and they meant a lot to me. Everyone said it was the most beautiful and equally sad funeral.

Hayley

Over the next few months Armand and I kept busy, he was back at work and I'd go to see my Mum and kept busy at home.

We had two meetings at Taunton hospital, to collect a memory box of Freya's things, ask questions, talk about Freya's final days and discuss the timing of having another baby.

Some people might not understand how you can already be talking and discussing having another baby after losing one, but our arms and hearts were empty and trying again was what we knew would help us heal.

No baby could ever replace Freya or take away the love, the memories and the pain of saying goodbye to her.

By July I was unexpectedly pregnant! I was happy and worried. Was it too soon? Had we grieved enough? Would enough time ever have passed though? Was my body going to be OK and would I be able to have a natural birth?

What would people think?

Armand was surprised but happy and not worried at all. He was a bit disappointed we wouldn't need to try! Hahaha!

We kept the news pretty quiet, my Mum and a few others had guessed, and we announced to my family in September just as my Dad got taken into hospital.

Sadly, I don't know if my Dad fully knew I was pregnant or not, as he was quite unwell and then passed away a few weeks later, which was very hard to go through whilst pregnant and five months after losing Freya.

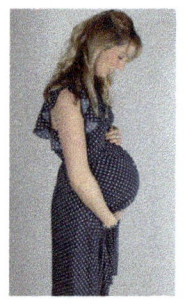

On Halloween we had our 20 week scan and found out it was another little girl, which we both were hoping for. Both of us were happy!

I was nervous about going back to work and also telling them I was pregnant again, but my boss was fine.

My pregnancy went well, I was healthy, eating well and I hired a doula (a non medical birth support person) to help me feel relaxed and to be at the birth supporting us both. I went to a pregnancy relaxation course for six weeks and made lots of my own affirmation cards.

Hayley

I was being seen by a consultant monthly from twenty weeks, having extra scans and all was going well. I was glad to be seen regularly and know our baby girl was fine, but I still had anxiety and knew I wouldn't feel completely relaxed until she was born and I knew she was OK. I was put on medication from 29 weeks to make sure baby didn't catch what Freya had and I took a homeopathic remedy, and a supplement too. I was making sure to cover all bases.

Going on maternity leave and then having my baby shower were all milestones that I never got to with Freya, which was very emotional. I held my baby shower at home - Armand and I put up lots of decorations the night before and it was a lovely day.

The last few weeks were ticking by and we were getting more and more excited wondering when would I go into labour, what the birth would be like, and who she would look like. I'd had my hospital bags packed for some months in anticipation in case I went into labour early again. I was going for walks, kerb walking, and eating lots of dates and relaxing! I just wanted her here now so I could relax.

I wanted to keep pain management as natural and drug free as possible so it didn't affect baby, and I'd planned to have a water birth.

On Thursday 20th March, Armand and I had a midwife appointment, I was forty weeks and five days. I was so happy I'd made it full term and the midwife was pleased with how I was and baby in position, but still no lower.

We went home and I did more kerb walking trying to get baby more engaged, we had a chilled day, relaxing around the house and watched some TV in the evening. Armand played the crystal and Tibetan bowls whilst I lay on the sofa for a bit as I found it so relaxing. At around 12.20am I woke suddenly - my waters had broken.

I woke Armand and called my doula. I took some homeopathic remedies, drank water, trying to ride the waves. We called an ambulance and our doula got to us quickly as my labour was progressing quickly, and I didn't think we'd make the drive.

Into the ambulance - we headed to Taunton hospital and twenty minutes after arriving at the hospital our beautiful daughter, 'Frieda Freya' was born naturally, on 21st March 2025 with the help of an episiotomy, my TENs machine, gas and air, and lots of determination!

Armand was by my side holding my hand and my doula was on the other side, plus 2 amazing midwives who respected my decisions. Frieda had arrived, healthy and well and I'd done it!

We had a few golden hours, uninterrupted, skin to skin time and established breast feeding. I was on cloud nine. I was ecstatic!

She's so beautiful, and Armand was so happy and having skin to skin cuddles with her with a big grin on his face. He told me later that day that he had left the room after she was born as he was feeling so emotional.

The last 4 months since Frieda was born have been amazing. Every day I feel so happy and grateful to be her Mum, for her to be our beautiful healthy daughter. Being a Mum is the best job in the world, I knew I would love it and it's what I'm here for. I get many tears of happiness just looking at her and thinking how lucky we are to have her and be parents. Our wish granted.

Of course there are the sleepless nights, breastfeeding through the night and sometimes feeling exhausted, but it's all worth it! Mum comes to stay for the odd night to help me and my doulas come to see how I'm doing.

For now, we are enjoying our bubble of love with 'Miss Frieda' and enjoying all our firsts. First time swimming, first holiday, first roll over the other day and she's just met her Latvian Grandad for the first time.

Our post-Covid years have been a bit of a rrollercoaster, but here and now, we are very happy parents planning all our new adventures with our precious daughter!

Susan from Northern Ireland

Back in 2023, many astrologers, psychics, remote viewers and channelers were telling us via their various online platforms, that the year 2024 was going to be pivotal in terms of massive changes taking place right across the world.

A revelation of the deceit, lies, hypocrisy and corruption behind all government, media and many large scale institutions will be so great, as to kick start a huge shift in the collective consciousness from all nations – a tipping point to mark the start of the onset of revolution!

Such was my curiosity, that I decided I'd record my perceptions, emotions and state of wellbeing on a monthly basis, to gauge the level of potential truth behind these prophecies. I was drawn once more to my newfound hobby of poetry writing – a creative outlet I'd discovered during lockdown.

There are clearly systems that can no longer be viewed as sustainable and are beginning to collapse. From this point on we may be in for a bumpy ride!

My poems illustrate how I have tried to prepare myself to face the next stage of this spiritual war, even though I really don't know what lies ahead. The following are some of my poems...

'I'M SO WEARY NOW'
November 2023

Those media puppets won't stop pushing fear
Who's now still listening, it doesn't seem clear
How many like me are sick of their games
I see right through them, I know their names
I want them and their masters removed from the earth
And abundance and beauty allowed to rebirth
They planned to enslave me with no freedoms left
But I know their playbook, so good luck with that quest
They can't control souls connected to Source
But keeping on trying is their mission of course
I'm so weary now but I mustn't give in
For I know in my heart that they never can win
It's lasted so long now; I must keep up the fight
Through their dark agendas, I'll shine my light
What gives them the right to have global control
Those power hungry villains who have no soul
I'm just so weary now, when will it end?
For, on days I feel sad, it's hard to pretend.

'MY WEARINESS IS LIFTING'
December 2023

I'm much brighter now, got back on my horse
Protected by armour, I'm now back on course
My armour's my courage, my wisdom my sword
I'm saving myself now, I give me my word
It's an inside job, my inner house to deep-clean
Then the outer world's sickness just has to be seen
The true path ahead is a spiritual one
The hero's journey we must make alone
Those parasitical occultists can't be our masters
When we know how they manipulate their constant disasters
They tried hard to divide us so we couldn't unite
But coming together, our light will shine bright
What's the point of us being here if we don't get to know
That we're all here to learn, to evolve and to grow
Find our piece of the puzzle in the grand game of life
Survive those tough challenges, heal from great strife
We understand our folly in relinquishing our power
To those global elitists who can't sink any lower
Perhaps the hardest challenge is learning to forgive
And priority for all mankind - upgrading how we live
They'll have to meet their maker, where God decides their fate
Their mission to enslave us, for them it's much too late
However long it has to take, one day nations will be free
To live, the lives we're meant to live in peace and harmony.

'EARTH SCHOOL'
January 2024

It's been the Devil's playground here on earth now for too long
The mission of dark agenda evil ones; our misery to prolong
Did we really choose this planet to be challenged by Earth School
Why commit to such harsh lessons, encounter much that seems
    so cruel
Strong, brave and curious students signed up for such a stint
Some questioning their soul contracts, should've scrutinized
    small print
As we only start to graduate when we accept that life is tough
Accept suffering put before us, cope when things get rough
Our unique life paths are full of tests, each offering something new
In every stage of evolution, many a personal vital clue
Bestowed from higher realms, however they're defined
We can really trust the source, as it's benevolent and kind
The most enormous test for us to dare to even comprehend
Is to learn our history's upside down and our governments
    aren't our friend
To know we're here to solve life's mysteries and to find out
    what to do
Investigate in what makes sense; with guidance, learn what's true
The shocking truth emerging is that earth has reached a phase
Where we can choose a path to freedom or stay imprisoned
    in a maze
In fear we stay in prison, when more enlightened we break free
With heart-centred intuition all deception we will see
We can recognise the movie is now coming to an end
To the cast of such bad actors, this message we can send
Don't offend us with your presence, we don't need to be polite
You cannot destroy our spirit as we're warriors of light!

'WHAT DOES IT MEAN TO BE FREE?'
April 2024

As I ponder on this question of what it means to be free
To provide a definitive answer seems an impossibility
Like balancing on a high wire, maintaining freedom feels the same
A constant reevaluation of how I understand the game
Of the globalists and their agendas to whom we're just debt slaves
Though I continually remind myself that no respect to them I gave
A thorough reassessment of whether I should listen to them lie
Or drown out their noise completely, to their demands just
    don't comply
I can call to mind some basic truths my soul has helped
    me understand
A reminder through my spiritual growth that I've the upper hand
Those globalists who have no soul can never capture mine
For on my sacred journey, I'm in harmony with the Divine
With this in mind, there's peace to find in many simplistic ways
A stimulating walk in nature; being by the sea, can elevate my days
Sitting quietly in meditation or finding creative things to do
Is perhaps what truly sets me free, this just feels to me so true
Then I get pulled back into the madness, there's really no escape
But if I really can't make sense of it, little notice I should take
At least it shouldn't overpower me and let it really cause me harm
I know that's the intention, to cause more chaos and alarm
How much of this is meant for those who understand these
    games of war
But more for those who've still to learn what all this mayhem's for
To help them see how foolishly they'd be giving away their power
If they don't protect their freedoms when it comes the critical hour

Put no more faith in psychopaths with their corruption for all to see
It's time to walk the spiritual path, to be fully alive and free
Self-healing is essential, a new attitude of mind

Susan from Northern Ireland

Reclaim the truth of our magnificence, leave limiting
    beliefs behind
How challenging the journey and how long it has to take
Depends on how we bravely come together and commitments
    we can make
It's our duty to ourselves and then to all mankind
To work side by side in harmony then great changes we may find
Like me, others may be struggling with what our supportive
    roles should be
I want to help create a better world for everyone, including me
We've all something to offer with unique experiences, talents
    and skills
There are many different tasks to choose and essential roles to fill
As a quiet and private woman, I often feel inadequate in this fight
I'm not an activist by nature; no social media platform or website
However, through people I have followed and books that I
    have read
I find that those pursuing their spiritual path offer something
    else instead
A spiritual and information war is what we're living through
Good against evil, dark against light, discerning what feels true
It's a wondrous revelation, a great joy to realise
We've everything we need within us, at our core we're really wise
Warriors who came before said freedom's not something others
    can impart
Awarded by outside controlling forces who pretend they
    have a heart
But rather something we are born with as a natural inalienable right
When enough of us believe this truth, we'll get stronger in the fight
Now I've asked myself this question of what freedom means to me
And I've considered many angles and this is what I really see
That no matter how the madness is going to prolong
No-one can take away my freedom as it's been there all along!

'GROUNDHOG DAY'
June 2024

From where things stand in present times, it's useful to reflect
On when and how did this deep attack on us commence
When was I convinced that our freedom's under threat
When news from media sources completely made no sense
To whip up intense fear, have people doubt they would survive
Was definitely the intention for each day
Of abusing forces that didn't want to see us thrive
Very deep and dark agendas were at play
Considering how I built up my protection during this harsh time
Looking back from 4 years on I feel some pride
I wonder whether others created strategies similar to mine
And not bowed down to corrupt people who had lied
Although, of course, it wasn't easy and often very tough
Anxiety and stress levels very high
Sometimes I felt so lost and completely had enough
And sought a safe, quiet and pleasant place to cry
Had others, like me, shared a similar sense of gloom
At the start of every day when the world was still the same
Preferred to pull over the covers, stay shielded in my room
Than willingly face up to all that madness once again
I would rarely jump up out of bed feeling fresh as a daisy
But wished a spaceship would come and carry me away
Did I want to still exist in a world that was so crazy
That was the serious challenge that met me every day

Each new dawn felt like 'Groundhog Day'; here we go again
This daunting pattern I woke up with grew and grew
But from deep inside I realised I could still ignite a flame
Create my own resilience and shift to something new
Replacing too much negativity with a good self-help routine
And morning rituals that empowered me; I'd be more joyous and at peace
Singing favourite songs while showering even helped to set the scene
For a much more structured day when tensions I'd release
Much kind and loving self-talk is another therapeutic tool
Repeated mantras that uplift me can be very powerful too
Commitment to them daily has become my golden rule
And with practice over time, this gets easier to do
I like saying affirmations that really strike a chord
I recite them very often and my favourite one must be
The one that touches me emotionally and offers most reward
- 'I AM HEALTHY, WEALTHY, WHOLE, SAFE AND FREE'.

'BEYOND THE MADNESS'
July 2024

Although, of course, life may still present a heavy challenge
With my patience often times wearing very thin
It mightn't take too much to knock me off my balance
If with a cheerful outlook I don't each day begin
But a much bigger picture I now more easily see
As an impartial observer, I'm studying the game
It's peaceful rebellion we're needing and not World War III
A threat those evil wizards keep trying to maintain
Take notice of the irony behind what we are being told
These globalist, elitist controllers have become a laughingstock
Lies, plots, schemes and scandals are rapidly being exposed
They're just pathetic puppets, fair game for us to mock
So, I'm cautiously optimistic, I see people standing tall
People power – It matters, the tyranny must end
Say 'No' to all dictators, see their institutions fall
Loud and wide across the world, this message we must send
I see it all as theatre; bad actors swapping roles and scripts
But the lights are on, I see the scenery falling down
An embarrassing fiasco is what this all depicts
Masks are slipping, make-up's running, each looking like a clown
They must obey their puppet masters, repeat the lines they're told to say
All that scary nonsense they still want us to believe
But their influence on the audience quickly fades away

Susan from Northern Ireland

In great numbers they decide it's time for them leave
To use the metaphor of theatre to work out what feels true
Intrigues me greatly, as I wonder whether any part of this is fact
Are world events a kind of movie put in front of me and you
To slowly wake us from our slumber and gauge how we react
If so, who would be controlling this game of mastermind
A secret counterforce perhaps, opposing a New World Order pact
Assisting the Great Awakening, the liberation of mankind
By helping us to comprehend the depth we've been attacked
The world's turned upside down and inside out, it's obvious by now
It's difficult to know the good guys from the bad
Little point in trying to figure out the who and what and how
The wheel of fortune flips again, then the world won't be as mad
The movie has to run its course, although it makes no sense
But to overthrow the enemy is something each of us should do
By shining light upon the world our support will be immense
Without fear, trust God's plan and our faith will see us through.

Alison from Brightlingsea, UK

Our Tribute to Mick

At the time of writing, it has been over three years since I lost my husband, Mick, and my children lost their father with covid. We are a close family and as a mother I have tried to be strong and support my children as best I can. I am so very proud of my daughter, Kayleigh and my son Chris, they have shown such courage and fortitude in coming to terms with the loss of their father in such difficult circumstances.

I would like to thank Rosanne for giving me another opportunity to write about Mick and how life has moved on. I would like to pay tribute to Mick who left us so suddenly. To lose a loved one is devastating, but not to be with them and say goodbye makes everything so much harder.

Alison from Brightlingsea, UK

In Book 3, I described Mick's admission to hospital at a time when the country was in the grips of the covid pandemic and the lockdown with its far-reaching, and sometimes nonsensical restrictions. Hospitals adopted a no visitor policy that was strictly adhered to. This meant our family and so many other families would not be given the chance to say goodbye.

Three years on, the rawness has subsided. Time doesn't necessarily heal, but time softens the pain like a stone worn smooth by the relentless action of the waves. Time eases the grief and allows us to remember loved ones through cherished memories without the gnawing grief and sadness.

How would I describe Mick? He was a kind, generous man with a dry sense of humour. He was quiet and reserved, enjoying a 'proper pint' at the local pub; he was a real ale man, just watching the world go by. He loved his family and we could always rely on him. He would do anything for his family, even if this meant time spent on the driveway on Christmas Day fitting a car part, which had been a Christmas present, to Chris's car. Mick was a car mechanic, and being very practical could turn his hand to most things. I miss his practical skills, luckily Chris has inherited his father's DIY skills and I can always turn to him for help.

Chris remembers from the time he could ride a motorbike and drive a car, his Dad was always on hand to sort mechanical issues. These invariably were never straightforward, engine rebuilds included. Mick having given matters 'a good course of thinking about' would set to and get the bike or car running within Chris's timeframe which was 'sharpish'.

Since Mick's passing, Father's Day has been understandably difficult. However, Kayleigh and Chris decided it should be a celebration, and each year they always meet up and have a picnic along with a photo of their Dad, enjoying each other's company and sharing memories.

Life has a way of prompting us to remember our loved ones. When I'm out walking and see a dog rose, it reminds me of Mick, he used to like them. Sometimes a Pink Floyd track randomly plays on the radio and that always reminds us of Mick.

With this in mind, when I see birds on the wing, to me they are the epitome of a free spirit. Red kites grace the skies where my daughter lives.

Such beautiful birds soar unencumbered on the thermals, we can only admire and envy their freedom as they survey all below them. So often when we are chatting about Mick, something compels us to look to the skies, and there will be a red kite flying over us. I like to think of Mick in spirit, free from earthly trappings watching over us.

Mick was a keen biker and I was totally in awe of his ability, so natural. With great trepidation, being somewhat vertically challenged, I passed my big bike test. I still remember the look on Mick's face when I announced 'we' should explore Scotland on our bikes. Mick agreed, praying for good weather. Scottish weather is notorious, and this was the start of many motorbike adventures we shared,

touring Scotland and Europe. Navigation would sometimes go awry, but quite often that wrong turning would lead to a beautiful and remote place that would become etched in our minds. This country has breathtaking scenery and I'm so glad we were able to make such lovely memories and be part of it.

Alison from Brightlingsea, UK

Our tribute to Mick wouldn't be complete if I didn't mention our dear labrador Archie. In 2014 we bought this chubby little puppy home, and life changed. We swapped the freedom of our motorbikes for the comfort of four wheels and refuge from the 'four seasons in one day' Scottish weather.

Our trips to Scotland always included a stopover at St Abbs, a childhood haunt for Mick. There is something about this place unaffected by the passage of time, nothing changes. Archie loves to swim at Coldingham Bay by the harbour, far too cold for me. When Mick recalled his childhood holidays swimming at this beach it was never cold or windy. I suspect it was regularly both, given the North Sea.

Every time we went up north Archie came too, he is widely travelled. I was chief route planner which invariably included a mountain hike or 'munro' as they say in Scotland.

I would be ahead, but Archie would always double back to check that Mick was making steady progress, then run to catch me up. What could be seen as a lack of ascending enthusiasm from Mick, was more than made up for by his descending enthusiasm which could be quite athletic and agile, probably fuelled by the local pub coming into view and that 'proper pint'.

Mick often said I'd dragged him up another mountain, but I really believe the view of the snow-capped mountains all the way to the Isle of Skye more than made up for it.

Archie has aged more than his years would suggest. He has arthritis largely due to genetics, but he is a real trooper and braves his old age with stoism. He is my best mate of over ten years and the dearest lad.

In my previous account I expressed my anger at the policies dreamt up by our government in an attempt to control the pandemic, and our lives when we needed the support of close family and friends. Following on from Mick's passing, can I forgive our government partying at a time when so many were in the throes of unimaginable grief and loss? Anger can only exert its power temporarily. What does it achieve apart from eroding our spirit? I cannot forgive, but I have to let the anger go now.

All this time later I have come to believe that the policies implemented by governments globally were never going to work in limiting the spread of an airborne virus. What did work was the fear campaign that was relentlessly forced upon the people. Fear and isolation makes us vulnerable at a time when we need the comfort of others. I also believe that gradually the truth is coming out and perhaps in the event of another pandemic, we will unite, standing firm to protect our freedoms.

Life moves on, but we will never forget our loved ones. They reside in our hearts and the very act of remembering them brings them close, surrounding us with love and comfort, loved ones never truly leave us.

Every story should have a happy ending and my story is no exception, as the old adage says "When one door closes, another one opens" and so often this is true, even if it takes a little while.

On 16th December last year, I welcomed my beautiful granddaughter, Mia into the world, she was so longed for and is so special. Kayleigh is a wonderful, devoted mother and her partner, Paul has embraced fatherhood.

Chris is absolutely thrilled to be an uncle and will be a big part of her life.

Kayleigh has designed a wonderful scrapbook for baby Mia. It is a moving tribute to her Dad and is a lovely collection of photos, words and phrases Mick used, so typical of his sense of humour. When Mia grows up, the scrapbook will be passed down to her and she will come to know her Grandad through these words and pictures, and listening to the shared family memories.

I am quite sure that Mick will be watching over his granddaughter with so much love and will always be walking beside her.

Mick, when you're not enjoying that "proper pint" as you would say, keep riding your motorbike along Heaven's highways - a true free spirit. Cheers Mick.

Zizi

Grounded by a Mask

My father lives in Marbella, in the southwest of Spain. As he's now in his 80s and travels less frequently, I don't get to see him often. So, in December 2019, I booked a flight with EasyJet from Bristol to Gibraltar to visit him and my stepmother. The date was set for Tuesday, 24th March 2020.

In February 2020, I travelled to London to attend a friend's funeral. It was there that I first heard people talking seriously about 'lockdowns' and the government potentially restricting movement. I laughed it off, it just seemed absurd – completely unheard of.

By mid-March, I began to suspect I wouldn't be able to fly to Spain. Although part of me still doubted lockdown would actually happen, the rising fear and intensity of the media coverage made me uneasy. I started to think, what if we really are in danger?

When the government announced that all travel abroad was cancelled and a national lockdown would begin, I was devastated. My father had just turned 82, and I hadn't seen him in over a year.

Despite my feelings, something didn't sit right with me. I found it hard to accept that we were being told we couldn't leave our homes or go to work. I began turning to alternative media for other perspectives, and came across reports that COVID-19 had been removed from the list of high consequence infectious diseases just days before lockdown began. That marked a turning point for me. I started to do my own research and question what was really going on.

I work at a school for children with social, emotional, and mental health difficulties. Initially, our school was closed to all staff and students. Given the nature of our work, safeguarding and maintaining contact with families remained essential.

After a few weeks, we reopened with skeleton staff and part-time rotas for students. The Department for Education advised that special schools should remain open – and we did, throughout all 2020 lockdowns. In truth, I was glad to return to work. It gave me a legitimate reason to leave the house, and I continued living my life freely. I didn't agree with the austere restrictions and chose not to comply with rules I felt infringed on my rights.

After the March 2020 flight was cancelled, I contacted EasyJet, who advised me to rebook. I did – several times – but each new flight was cancelled. Finally, I managed to book a flight to Gibraltar for 27th June 2021, over a year later.

I drove to Bristol Airport for a 6am flight, arriving around 4am. The airport was eerily empty. Only two flights were scheduled that morning, mine and another to Poland. There were no other flights out of Bristol Airport until the afternoon.

EasyJet had a policy requiring all passengers to wear face masks. I'd never worn a mask during COVID, as I didn't believe a thin layer of fabric or paper provides meaningful protection from a virus. Still, I brought one with me just in case. I passed through check-in and security without issue, although I did notice six heavily armed Border Force officers in the departure area, questioning passengers about where they were going, intimidating, to say the least.

As I waited to board, a young EasyJet ground crew member questioned me about wearing a mask. I told him I was filming our interaction, which he didn't like. He insisted I wear a mask on the plane, and I asked if I could remove it to eat and drink – he said yes.

At the final boarding gate, another staff member told me my fabric mask was not acceptable. A fellow passenger kindly offered me a surgical-style mask, which I put on. I proceeded outside towards the plane. Suddenly, the young man from earlier marched toward me, saying aggressively, "You're not getting on this plane. Follow me." I continued walking, assuming he wasn't serious, but he returned with another staff member and physically escorted me away from the boarding area. He claimed he had told the captain I refused to wear a mask – despite the fact I was wearing one at the time.

They removed my suitcase from the hold, delaying the flight. I was taken back to a deserted departure hall, where I waited alone for my luggage. I tried calling the parking company, but they weren't answering – it was too early, and I wasn't due back for three days. Eventually, a member of the ground crew brought me my bag and apologised. He said this shouldn't have happened but that there was nothing he could do. It was clear that my challenge to the staff member – questioning his authority and citing my rights had cost me my seat.

I called my partner at 6am to come and pick me up, leaving my car behind until the parking company reopened the next day.

I emailed EasyJet's customer service and copied in the CEO. Within 20 minutes, I received a call. I explained everything and requested a refund, since I was denied travel. They initially refused, claiming I had agreed to their face mask policy. I pointed out that no such policy existed when I booked the ticket in 2019.

After two days of back-and-forth, EasyJet agreed to rebook me on another flight to Málaga, but they would not issue a refund. Though I had no desire to fly with them again, I accepted their offer and finally travelled to see my father.

The whole experience was unnecessarily traumatic - for both me and my father, and entirely avoidable. One young man decided I wasn't fit to fly, even though I complied with the rules. His decision separated me from my elderly father for yet another stretch of time.

When I look back now, I cannot believe what happened to me, could have happened!

Fortunately since 2022, I have been able to travel regularly to visit my father who is now 86 years old, but we will always look back at this time with horror and disbelief.

JB

I walked a mile
Behind a smile
I think I've done OK
From here to there
Without a care
I've chased the miles away
I've ducked I've dived
To survive
The pitfalls in the road
Each step you take
Can make or break
Increase or lighten the load
Many traps are set
You know just what I mean
I fell in a few
And so did you
None of them foreseen
You walk the walk
You talk the talk
Feeling so serene
But life is short
And you've been caught
A mile or two downstream
You clamber out
You scream and shout
Then you feel OK
So walk a mile
Behind a smile
Today's your lucky day.

Deborah Jane Sutton

I love this account - 'Memories of Lockdown' - of our evolution at this time of The Great Awakening which, for many of us really kicked in during 2020.

I continue to study energy and develop my understanding of how we create our own reality.

It makes sense to me that if we want to create a better future, we must first understand how we have created the reality we presently have.

I have found a lot of the answers to my many questions in the book 'Kybalion' written in 1908, by the Three Initiates which outlines the 7 Hermetic Principles. These 7 principles are the laws that govern the Universe and the workings of the Universe.

The 2nd of these principles is The Principle of Correspondence which states "As Within, So Without, As Above, So Below." It makes it clear that what we perceive as being 'outside' of us, is in fact a holographic projection of our own energy – warts and all!!

The World is a giant mirror. When we can get out of denial about this principle, we can work with our triggers and judgements and transmute our own darkness into love. Fill your field with the frequency of love, for everyone and everything, and this Love will get mirrored back to you. This is how we create a more loving world for ourselves and for the collective.

Understanding that we are multi-dimensional Light Beings really helps too. Realising that our physical world, and our physical bodies, are created from the frequency of our emotional and mental energy bodies, really helps us see the power and importance of emotional healing and mastering our thoughts. I enjoy sharing and simplifying these principles through my Workshops, Talks, Coaching and videos on YouTube where I, not only share weekly and monthly Energy Updates and Messages through Tarot but I also have a series on 'Lessons in Awakening' to help others understand these life-changing concepts.

I continue to run The Garden Retreat in Pego, Costa Blanca, Spain where I offer my own Workshops, Readings, Healings and Teachings as well as host Events and Workshops for others.

I am passionate about helping other passionate people get their gifts 'out there' to our Community.

It is a growing Community. A Community focused on Love. Love for ourselves, Love for each other and Love for Humanity. A Community governed by Love and Kindness. Sharing and Support. Learning, Growing, Evolving, as, together, we create 'The New Earth'.

Here are some 'realisations' that have helped me the most:

'Love is Everything and Everything is Love'.

'When you are busy creating the New, fighting the old becomes irrelevant.'

'If you want to create a better reality for yourself and the collective, your commitment to creating the New must be greater than your attachment to the old.'

'The only thing I can do for you is to work on myself and the only thing you can do for me is to work on yourself.'

'I am not what you think I am. YOU are what you think I am.'

'The future does not exist except for a thought in your head. If you don't like the look of your future, change the thought in your head.'

'There is not just one world. We are all creating our own world. When you stop focusing on the old and unpreferred, and spend your time creating what your heart is inspired to do, you will soon see a change in your reality and the world around you.'

Love and Blessings,

Deborah Jane Sutton

www.deborahjanesutton.com

Barbara and Derek Ponsford

Well here I am sitting in the same chair at the same table as I was in August 2023. Have two years really passed? Last night I re-read our story from 2023 and much of it feels very 'Deja Vu'.

However, two years really have passed and in that time we have had some highs and some lows, some happy and some sad times. We have had visits from our daughters and son-in-law and we've had holidays in Greece, we've had more adventures on our Yellow Board outings and with our Stand In The Park group. We've watched world events and sat in wonder and despair, and we've questioned 'Freedom'.

We've experienced the sadness of losing dear friends and the tragic loss of a tiny precious life. We've celebrated our Golden wedding anniversary and I have had my 80th birthday, and so we will take this opportunity to tell you about all of this...

In our previous stories I have written about how much we enjoy our trips out with the 'Yellow Boards', and so to a recent trip... We did our Outreach at a local town's independent market, where there were huge crowds attending, situating ourselves at the bottom of the town, about 15 of us stood with our boards, leaflets and 'The Light' paper.

Most of us could not believe the abuse we were still receiving after 4 plus years. People querying why I was holding a board with the words 'Justice for the vaccine injured'. Steve's board with the words 'Why are the vaccinated still getting sick with Covid?' and Derek's board said 'Keep Cash. Use it or Lose it'. We also had hanging boards saying 'Digital ID. No Freedom' and '15 minute cities will destroy Freedom'.

People were passing by and still hurling abuse at us, telling us to get ourselves educated and calling us stupid idiots, perhaps we need to be on medication. Most won't engage in discussing the very concerning issues we raise, so we do believe with the next 'Plandemic', people will still comply, which is a HUGE worry to us.

On a more positive note, many people did engage with us, thanking us and saying how much they are with us. I also had a lady ask me about my 'Vaccine Injuries Board', and it was good we could advise her on how she may be able to help her friend who had suffered a brain bleed shortly after his jab - 55 years old and his life ruined forever.

People were coming up to us saying how much they appreciated what we were doing and they were wholeheartedly with us. People talked to us about their friends, or friends of friends who were vaccine damaged, and had lost their work and way of life because of the damage, and some had 'lost' a loved one.

One lady said she'd lost both her brothers, both were fit and healthy before they had their vaccines.

At the end of that positive afternoon we felt uplifted and felt we really were making a difference, so nine or ten of us went and had a drink together - a nice way to finish the day.

In December 2024 we went to Glastonbury to an event organised by Rosanne; we were particularly interested to hear Andrew Bridgen talk as he has spoken out consistently over the past years for the vaccine damaged. We really admire  him and were so pleased to not only meet him, but to have a photo taken of us with him - one of our heroes of today.

Lots of thumbs up!
At an event last week we had a really positive response - I carried my 'Justice for the vaccine injured' board. Steve's board drew attention to 'Chemtrails' and Derek's board said 'Vaccines 2024', and a Henry Kissinger quote: "Once the herd accepts mandatory forcible vaccination, it's game over! They will accept anything – forcible blood or organ donation – for the 'greater good'. We can genetically modify children and sterilise them – for the 'greater good'. Control sheep minds and you control the herd. Vaccine makers stand to make billions, and many of you in this room today are investors. It's a big win-win! We thin out the herd and the herd pays us for providing extermination services."

So to this last couple of years... it has been very mixed with some really good times and some not so good ones.

We still do 'Stand In The Park' most Sundays. We still believe it to be an excellent way for people to connect and we have found some wonderful life long friends through our local SITP.

Sadly, as with many groups, it can also become divisive, which has happened at many Stands including ours. When speaking to people from other Stands, it always seems to be ego or money which rears its ugly head and causes the divisions. Derek and I find this very sad as in our early days it was the best place ever.

In April 2024 I celebrated my 80th birthday and Derek and I took ourselves off to Christchurch in Dorset for a couple of nights in a hotel. We had a lovely time and although our daughters both live far away, a friend of our younger daughter came and met us on my birthday which was lovely.

Although my birthday was joyful, it was also tinged with great sadness due to a devastating loss, which will be something I will reflect on every 11th April.

In May 2024 we had some wonderful news from our eldest daughter, Trudi, and son-in-law, Richard; they were coming back from Australia for a visit in June, it was their first trip to the UK in almost 19 years, and we were overjoyed. Unfortunately they hadn't checked dates with us first and we missed so many days of their visit because we were on holiday in Skiathos.

Their visit was short and sweet as they only came for two weeks and although it was disappointing to be away for part of the time they were visting, it was lovely to see them.

Our holiday - our first visit to Skiathos; we enjoyed another two glorious weeks, in Greece. The weather was gorgeous every single day and we stayed in a great hotel with yet again wonderful staff.

Our nightly visits to the different Tavernas were the highlight of our holiday! Fabulous food and the most wonderful Greek people - I never want to leave... We have already set our sights on visiting Crete next year!

We were delighted when we heard that our younger daughter, Kerry, was coming home for a week at the end of July 2024 for our Diamond wedding anniversary on the 1st August, as we had thought we would be spending it alone. We had a lovely few days with Kerry and on our anniversary we had a very happy day, part of it spent with a special friend, and in the evening we had a fabulous meal at a French Bistro in Sherborne. It really was a very special day - a day to remember!

We have been truly blessed with people's kindness, continuing our anniversary celebrations, being treated to meals out and coffees and cake to celebrate.

As I mentioned, there have been the not so good times as well. Sadly we have lost a number of friends over the last couple of years, and some we believe should still be here. In some cases we have learnt from their relatives that they had been put on end of life care which left us sad and doubtful. How can a person be eating meals, having a normal conversation and walking around one day, and in less than 24 hours be gone, having been put on end of life care. Not just one of our friends - it doesn't seem right.

I have been following Jacqui Deevoy for quite a while. Her stories on the administration of Midazolam and Morphine are quite horrendous during the Plandemic era... Can this still be going on now?

A little while ago, I read a post on Facebook asking why people were still doing 'Stand In The Park' and the 'Yellow Boards', handing out informative leaflets and 'The Light' newspaper giving alternative views and information. The tone of the post was quite aggressive, so I didn't reply, but the comment on 'how we still have Freedom' was mentioned which really made me think! Do we have Freedom?

Freedom... I thought back to 2004.

We had just celebrated our Ruby anniversary and some friends, Peter and Helen, took us on holiday with them, touring France and Belgium. Peter had planned the whole tour and he had planned it well, it was a lovely holiday and we did and saw some wonderful things. The days I remember most are our visits to Tyne Cot Memorial and Thiepval Memorial. The emotion of seeing all those white headstones of unknown soldiers, and such young ages. The only sound you could hear was our sobbing as we stood there with tears streaming down our faces. All I could think of was how they had died for us to be here today. They gave us Freedom... We also went to Menin Gate to listen to the 'Last Post'. It was a weekday evening and there were hundreds of people there; again the tears fell.

My Dad was one of thirteen children and sadly one of his brothers died in Malta in World War II. He was only in his early twenties and my Gran grieved for him every day until her death. These young men fought for our 'Freedom'.

Right now there is still so much tyranny in place and our right to free speech is rapidly disappearing, so many other things happening right across the world, we are losing our Freedom. Can we really let my Uncle Arthur and those young soldiers lives be lost in vain...

For the last 5 years, we have been fighting for Freedom, fighting for our children, our grandchildren and our great grandchildren. We want them to have Freedom.

Freedom to travel, not be locked up in 15 minute cities, and do whatever they want to do, to eat whatever they want to, eat and not be controlled in any way.

Today, yet again I see everyone is posting and talking about 'Chemtrails'. The subject that is constantly dismissed, especially by our MPs, despite the fact that we are hearing more and more from countries across the world that are experiencing the same.

I'm up very early most mornings and during the summer months I look out at beautiful clear blue skies; I then watch up to 6 planes decimating the lovely sky with trails that turn the whole sky into a milky white colour, which stays for the rest of the day followed by rain. When is something going to be done about it?

I guess nothing will be done about it as we are told it is all about 'Climate Control'. Derek and several others have emailed our local MP asking, questioning him about the chemtrails and they all received the same standard email reply dismissing our concerns.

Recently, when talking to a few different friends about what is going on in the world, I was shocked to hear that none of them have heard of Klaus Schwab, the WEF, Davos etc. None of them are the least bit interested in knowing either.

Keeping cash, no Farmers no Food, disappearing bees - all things that mean so much to us. When they do 'wake up' - it could be too late!

Earlier I mentioned that we had celebrated our Diamond anniversary on 1st August 2024 - a very happy memory. A group of people from our 'Stand In The Park' got together and arranged a 'surprise belated Diamond anniversary party' for us on Saturday evening 31st August 2024. We were offered a lift to what we thought was a summer disco. We arrived to a beautifully decorated hall, a DJ started playing

'Congratulations' and a line of wonderful friends emerged to welcome us with big hugs. To say we were overwhelmed and emotional is an understatement. The amount of work, care, and kindness that had been put into our surprise party was amazing! So many lovely little touches, including a beautiful cake with our wedding photo on it.

Do you remember earlier in our story when we returned from Skiathos, we said we would visit Creat next year... well, we have just returned from a wonderful two weeks in Crete! We went to Chania on the recommendation of a friend who stayed there last year, we actually stayed in the same hotel and had the same room as she had stayed in the year before! We were, as ever, overwhelmed by the hospitality of the Greek people, the marvellous food they served us each night with such care and amidst happy chatter!

The weather - we had fourteen days of up to fifteen hours of beautiful clear blue skies each day - with no white lines turning them grey - absolutely gorgeous!

We spent our days between relaxing at the pool, catching a bus into the town centre to wander the pretty streets and the marina, before choosing which taverna to eat at in the evening. The old town of Chania was beautiful and we spent a relaxing day on the beach.

We enjoyed meeting and chatting to some lovely people, both local and others holidaying, and our hotel was really lovely; we had a garden room and enjoyed many an hour reading on our balcony which gave us welcome shade.

After our two fabulous weeks, we returned home feeling recharged and with healthy tans - we haven't decided where to head to next year!

I ended our last story trying to stay positive; we had hoped things would improve, but we don't feel they have. We avoid all news except the UK Column News.

We often discuss how have we lived so long and had not realised the depth of corruption throughout the world; we have become sceptical about every single thing now, and it doesn't feel good to be living like this.

For over three years, people have kept telling us life will be so good soon, that good things are coming, but we are wondering WHEN? Both in our 80s - we need the good things NOW!

Sara Appleton

In February 2020, there was speculation of this virus in China, and that it was headed our way.

My boyfriend chose the film 'Contagion' as our evening film, and looking back now, there were so many similarities of what followed.

Just a month later, the world closed its doors, shielded from an unknown virus filled with speculation.

I lived in a small Somerset town with my son aged 6 and our cat Lula. We lived in a two-bed house with a small garden and, looking back, we were lucky to have this space and location, giving us the freedom to talk and walk and enjoy the fresh air.

Firstly I was working at a local animal park and they were forced to shut the doors, leaving customers in limbo of their membership fees. Secondly, school shut, and they weren't really prepared for it.

With my work closing, they soon let me go, leaving me to scurry for a salary whilst homeschooling my child and, as the only money earner in the household, times were scary.

We were allowed to be in 'bubbles', ie. people who we could see from outside our home. Who you chose depended on whether they were in touch with others, as some people were 'key workers' which meant they continued working. I believe a bubble was allowed to be up to 6 people, from two different households.

My parents bubbled with our elderly grandmother so I chose to bubble with a friend and her two kids. This allowed us to go for walks together, although we still kept the 2 metre distance which was hard with 3 kids under the age of 7!

My boyfriend, who was considered a 'key worker' continued working. He had a manual job that carried on as normal and he distanced himself from us as he was at risk, working with 200+ people daily.

Initially we were told a lockdown of two weeks and this soon extended further; adapting to our new life within our walls and the uncertainty of how long this would last was hard.

Homeschooling was a battle, I'm not a teacher and the admiration for teachers soon grew! As a solo mum, searching for a job, the stress levels were high. Adding in the absence of my boyfriend, the only thing keeping me sane was the discovery of a Gin subscription box!

Don't get me wrong - we had funny, entertaining times. I put the tent in our back garden which just about stretched from one end to the other. I painted the fence and hired a pressure washer - the weather was wonderful and the garden looked the best it had in years! We had scavenger hunts around the house and did Zoom dance and fitness classes. I attended a virtual 40th birthday for a friend and learnt how to cut my son's hair!

I loved the community spirit that grew among the neighbours. Although we have a small shop in my town, the choice was limited and getting to a supermarket (with a 6 year old) would only put us at risk. So the neighbours all looked out for each other by gathering shopping requests when a supermarket delivery slot became available (they were in high demand, as you may expect!).

My neighbours are two single households, so we took to chatting over our fences, getting that social interaction whilst distanced. Going for a daily walk kept us active, and we soon discovered local walks on our doorstep and enjoyed the quiet of the local A road.

I can't remember every phase of the 'in lockdown' and 'out of lockdown', but I do remember how my son suffered missing his friends. The social contact was limited, and although we would go for walks with our bubble friends, it wasn't very much interaction.

At some point the school organised set Zoom sessions for learning, with tasks to complete in the week which helped, although my son hated being on camera and speaking up.

Being unemployed was hard. It was a time when people were urged to 'be kind' and I begged my employer to 'furlough' me.

To explain... the government introduced a scheme called the CJRS (Coronavirus Job Retention Scheme) in March 2020; this scheme provided grants to employers so they could retain and continue to pay staff during coronavirus related lockdowns, by furloughing employees at up to 80% of their wages.

My employer declined and, to this day, I refuse to give that business any of my money as I felt an injustice, I couldn't understand why they'd refuse.

My saving grace was being able to claim furlough through my previous business which I ran as a limited company. I had traded in the years set in the criteria and was able to claim this with unemployment.

By early June, a friend had suggested I freelance, offering my marketing and admin knowledge to businesses to bring in some income. I started networking, virtually of course, and it wasn't long before I had my first client, and then my second. Fitting work around homeschooling and when my son was sleeping or occupied elsewhere.

We both had our vaccinations. The NHS staff were amazing, especially one particular doctor who eased my son's anxiety with his singing and ukelele playing - later instructing him to stand on the X on the floor - and as soon as you could blink, the vaccine had been applied. They even gave him a certificate and sticker as a well done.

I am still freelancing. Life as it was pre-Covid, slowly returned over perhaps two to three years. Although there is still a little remnant of that time whenever someone coughs, sneezes or wears a face mask.

We are frequent goers to music festivals - among a crowd yet more aware of keeping distances between people. There is still an element of personal space that lives past lockdown.

My son and I regularly talk about how lockdown was. There are a lot of good memories - his favourite being not having to go to school (as most kids, I suspect!). Walking and cycling, we remember the tranquility during lockdown. The queues to get into our local shop, limited to four at a time. The wearing a mask on a bus, even when we were the only ones on there.

They're all memories of a time that will always be a conversation point.

It's amazing how different countries responded to the outbreak of Covid and the lockdowns. How a split between the 'vaccinated' and the 'not vaccinated' developed, but what I do love is that everyone has their own story, each different, with fascinating memories of what it was like!

JB

Instinct

What is it? Does it work? Do you trust it?

It's that inner compass that can show you the way. It doesn't rely on logic. It senses the long view. Not quick fixes. It's not always pointing you in the safe direction, but encourages you to look deeper in your decision making. Key decisions such as your chosen workplace and the right life partner probably  determine future satisfaction and happiness. Things aren't always as they appear, and sometimes that inner voice seems to have second sight. But do you listen to it? Can you trust it? Well that requires some consideration and time for the inner clock to make its mind up and adjust expectations. Time is of the essence. A short term 'punt' could be fun and maybe you need that bit of 'fun', after all there are boxes that have to be ticked. Personal goals need to be scored. You don't want to end up with a list of 'if onlys'. But that inner instinct can get you back on track. But it's your choice. Ignore it at your peril. Anyway, good luck as you plan your way through the minefield called life. So **'set the controls for the heart of the sun'**. But don't fly too close.

Skye Coelho

As I looked back upon my last contribution to this book series, I was struck by how grim it seemed: illness, death, grief...

And then thought, blimey! Now I have to tell them what happened next and some of it ain't pretty!

However, in the darkness there is always light and I have some light to share too...

I write this in a lovely wooden house where we are currently pet sitting two adorable older dogs on Spain's Costa Blanca.

At the end of 2023 I spent time living and working at a cat and donkey sanctuary in the same area. Those of you who have read my previous contributions will remember my time living off-grid in various caravans so living in yet another caravan and surrounded by animals was a godsend particularly after my gruelling time in the UK.

During that period I decided to try an online dating site, a slightly different type to the norm (Spiritual Singles) and just test the waters... I chatted to a few interesting guys in various countries, but soon felt I wasn't ready nor in the right head space to connect, and so tried to delete my account. I clearly remember it being an issue and every time I tried to delete, something happened and just as I became really frustrated, a message dropped into my inbox and so Gabe entered my life...

Gabe, the Norwegian living in Denmark, arrived in Spain approximately 2 months later and stayed at the donkey sanctuary with me and the rest is history.

I went to Denmark three times to stay with him there and now he has left Denmark permanently to find a path forward here together. My visits to Denmark were very therapeutic for me; visiting some beautiful places, fully immersing ourselves in the Danish forests and learning to forage. I also began to learn to make tinctures from dandelions and nettles.

Throughout that period I had noticed some worrying symptoms including left hand tremors, dizzy spells, confusion, memory loss, swelling and many other symptoms: Long story short, I had developed severe adverse reactions to the antidepressants that I had been on for a year, which culminated in a brain hemorrhage and other unpleasant injuries... I have spent over a year recovering and through the use of plant medicine and various protocols, I am improving immensely to how I was. I reported all this to the

Pharmaceutical company concerned and the medical authorities, but that is a whole other story...

Meanwhile, Gabe and I began our own off-grid project with a bell tent and my caravan, first on the family land and now on a friend's land up in the mountains, back in the area where I lived in 2022.

At the moment we are living full time in only the bell tent, 6 metre diameter. We have our basic solar power and access to a tap! We made a basic compost toilet in a separate tent and have a shower tent with a big plastic bowl and some solar shower bags. Basic indeed.

We are also undertaking the renovation of my friend's 1999 Renault Kangoo, which has sat for 20 years in the scorching sun playing host to hundreds of wasps! We hope to restore it to its former glory and use it as a work and travel van.

So, on the bright side I have a wonderful partner who is on the same wave length as me, by my side to navigate our way forward in these turbulant times, both personal and global, and new adventures...

2020 was just the beginning of this particular chapter in human history. I believe there is way more to come. Funnily enough, whilst editing this last part, we experienced the 'blackout', grid down in Spain. This is something that has been warned about for many years, and whether it is viewed from a practical perspective regarding the vulnerability of the electrical grid, the possibilities of sabotage, or solar activity etc. etc., if anything, it showed a lot of people how much is taken for granted and how, in minutes, everyday life can descend into chaos... Despite living off-grid, the moment our phone lines went down I found myself in a moment of panic, the realisation that I could not call any family or friends to see if they were okay.

So, no matter how prepared we think we are, mentally and spiritually for more change and chaos, it still puts us to the test.

Of course there were nice anecdotes from those who found peace from the non-stop cycle of tech: families sitting down to play cards, reading, watching the sunset... a whole generation who had never experienced life before mobile phones and were momentarily liberated from non stop selfies and social media pressures... everything is a double-edged sword.

I have a new baby niece who brings much joy to the family, and so as I pointed out at the beginning, **'even in times of complex difficulties, there is Light and reasons for Gratitude.'**

Julie

Looking back over the last five years, my memories have been bittersweet; a mixture of emotional lows... painful and sad, together with feelings of loneliness, fear, frustration, and depression interspersed with pleasurable times and hours of heightened creativity. I learnt to make resin jewellery, crafts, fluid art, and painting terracotta pots, amongst other things.

During the first lockdown while living in Essex, I remember waking up every morning to glorious warm, sunny weather with beautiful clear blue skies. This was most unusual for March and seemed to continue for months. Most notably, the sky was silent apart from the birds flying freely in their rightful habitat and, more importantly, there were no signs of any air traffic or chemtrails!

Julie

I was furloughed for about six weeks and spent the majority of that time in hermit mode, feverishly researching everything 'covid' and lockdown related. At that time there was little to no censorship on social media platforms, therefore, I had access to lots of information and interviews featuring many respected doctors, scientists and virologists, etc. and I took off down many rabbit holes!

I arrived in Wiltshire in June 2020 having moved from Essex where I'd lived for the previous eleven years, seven of which were caring for my mum after my dad passed away in 2009. I continued to live in mum's house after she passed away in January 2016 for a further four years, but was finding it increasingly difficult to cope with my job and life in general. I ended up feeling desperate and burnt out. I didn't know what to do or how to move on as my share of the sale proceeds when the house was sold would not be enough to buy a home, and I was approaching retirement age with no prospect of securing a mortgage.

As a solution, my sister and brother-in-law invited me to live with them in Wiltshire in their annex which was such a relief. However, I found out much later that this was more a logical decision on their part and not really because they wanted me to live with them. I had sensed this from day one, which made my existence in those early months and years much more difficult, depressing, and fearful than they need have been. I felt unwanted and a burden but grateful for a temporary haven.

I had moved to a county where I knew no-one except my sister and brother-in-law, nephew and his family. My daughters lived miles away in London, and my friends nowhere near either. Eventually, through reaching out on Facebook, attending 'Stand in the Park' meetings, and later various talks, I met and made some lovely like-minded friends to chat and find refuge with.

Many seemed unaffected by the rules and regulations of 'Covid' (Certificate of Vaccination ID?) and lockdown. However, it brought devastation to many families and people of all ages. Money and health issues along with differing views and opinions created alienation, division, anger, loneliness, isolation, grief, despair, rejection, fear, hostility, violence, abuse, and even suicide/death. Was this all a plan to destroy the family unit and any sense of community, keeping us distracted and fighting each other, so we wouldn't work out what was really happening?

After talking to various family members, it became apparent I was the only one who could see through the lies and deception spewing 24/7 from the media. The pitch, speed and intensity at which newscasters spoke was enough to induce constant anxiety and fear in anyone! I was concerned for those who obsessively watched, absorbed and ultimately became, it seemed, brainwashed by this fear mongering. The 'trusted' BBC were the worst culprits with total censorship and suppression of any scientific debate. A voice was only given to approved agencies with no alternatives, such as expressed on social media platforms by real doctors and independent experts, truly concerned for, and questioning, the 'safety and effectiveness' of wearing masks, keeping six feet apart and the supposedly novel vaccines. Maybe the correct term is 'experimental gene-modifying injections' that could induce infertility (depopulation?) and cause more adverse reactions and deaths than all other vaccines put together - all for a ' virus' less lethal than seasonal flu and with a 99.98% recovery rate - absolutely bat crazy (excuse the pun!) and nothing short of MK Ultra mind control!

To my dismay my sister and brother-in-law had totally bought into the narrative. They did not believe or want to listen to what I had to say and they really didn't like me not conforming to the covid rules, mask wearing and lockdown. However, having studied and qualified in natural nutrition, I chose to believe terrain theory over germ theory. Something felt very wrong and, at its core, quite sinister. I felt so strongly about my views that I was not about to betray myself to please them or anyone else.

I remember the dreaded moment when masks were introduced as 'mandatory'. I was in my car in a Tesco car park with my heart pounding, plucking up the courage to face the two big burly security guards at the entrance. I knew I couldn't be prevented from entering the store because it was unlawful and a violation for any individual or business to ask for evidence of an exemption under the Equality Act 2010, but I was still full of dread. At that time, I was the only one in the store without a mask on… it seemed truly surreal!

When the 'vaccines' arrived I was even more fearful for the wellbeing and safety of my family. I practically begged my daughters not to have any, and prayed every day that they didn't. Five years on, I am so relieved to find out that one of my daughters did not have any, although I still do not know whether my other daughter did or not. As far as I know, most other family members did succumb.

Food for thought:
Many eminent doctors and naturopaths believe that viruses are not contagious and also contend that the only way to 'catch' a virus is to be injected with it. Another consideration may be that viruses are passed on through epigenetic changes and inheritance.

Dr Kary Mullis was the creator of the PCR test who conveniently died in August 2019 not long before the 'plandemic'. He stated: "With PCR, if you do it well, you can find anything in anybody." PCR uses amplification and that enlarging any molecule over 25 cycles will give a false positive. Globally, the tests have been run anywhere between 30 to 50+ cycles thereby producing very high false positive results. Apparently, even a paw paw tested positive according to the then Tanzanian President!

If the vaccines are so safe and effective, why were we being coerced, bribed or blackmailed into taking them, and if 'covid' was so deadly, why would you have to be tested to know you had it?

Why was all the blame being directed onto unvaccinated people? If the vaccines worked, why would unvaccinated people be a threat? Were people being brainwashed to be afraid of unvaccinated people as though they were the ones causing the 'virus' to spread? More division and alienation?

Why were unvaccinated people made to feel threatened by the shedding of the spike protein of vaccinated people?

If the vaccine was safe, then why was there a 'no liability clause' making it impossible to sue Big Pharma?

Why did Fauci warn us of a 'surprise outbreak' of infectious disease back in 2017? Did he know something we didn't?

Revelations 18-23: '…for by thy sorceries were all nations deceived.' The word 'sorceries' translates to the Greek word 'pharmakeia' which is the root of pharmaceutical. The verse implies that the 'sorcery' of Babylon in the end times will

likely include drug production and trafficking. The verse foresees a global misuse of drugs to bewitch and mislead all nations. Does this sound familiar?

In the early days especially, I felt very alone, unsupported, unheard, unvalued and afraid to speak out. I now feel sad and empty inside, although I still have compassion for anyone who succumbed to taking the injections believing the lies of the globalists, thinking they were doing the right and honourable thing. Some people still believe this as, so far, they are unharmed by them. However, we are told millions of people were and are still suffering, albeit under a different umbrella, with an increase in turbo cancers and autoimmune diseases, heart disease, myocarditis, blood clots, inflammation of the spinal cord, disabilities, facial paralysis, allergies, allergic reactions, seizures, anaphylactic shocks, strange aches and pains, swellings, inflammation, and coughs that won't go away, to mention only a few.

If you have been injured by these injections, there is much you can do to mitigate the effects, with many protocols now available and lots of new technologies and frequency based healing modalities that will be able to help you, together with changes in nutrition and lifestyle choices, etc.

The madness and craziness seems to be accelerating in the political arena and in the censorship of our rights and freedom of speech. Everything seems so fake and plastic, becoming more insane and ridiculous every day. It's so unbelievable and surreal, comical almost, if it wasn't so serious. What is real and authentic? Is reality crumbling? Is this all just theatre? Am I living in the twilight zone? Am I an avatar in a computer game or simulation? I feel like I'm living in a different world... just observing the insanity!

Have we all been the cleverly manipulated victims of one of the biggest ever psychological operations? A PSYOP that has been planned for decades and carried out in lockstep unity across the world which caught, it seems, the majority of its inhabitants completely unaware and unprepared. It is easy to see how both sides were played against each other, filling us full of fear, confusion, and division. A nation will concede to anything if they are frightened into giving their power away to be 'saved', in this case, by Big Pharma and the 'nanny state' which has been insidiously forming in the background for decades. Fear, division, anger, confusion and false hope works every time to our detriment and takes away our autonomy, power and freedom.

The bifurcation of humanity is becoming more evident between those who want to remain human and those who don't, and those who turn a blind eye or don't have eyes to see.

I am reminded of the film 'A Bug's Life' which could be construed as an analogy of what is happening in our current capitalist society: it's about the life of a young optimistic ant called Flik who leads a rebellion against the seemingly more powerful grasshopper overlords that feed on food harvested by the ants (us). Hopper (the leader) and his gang are actually locusts (cabal) but pretend to be grasshoppers (government) so as not to rouse suspicion towards other bugs. They are bullies, and Hopper works to maintain the 'illusion' of power. There is an apt part in the film where Hopper menacingly says: "You let one ant stand up to us, then they all might stand up. Those puny little ants outnumber us a hundred to one, and if they ever figure that out, there goes our way of LIFE! It's not about food, it's about keeping those ants in line. THAT'S why we're going BACK!"

Long story short, Flik courageously stood up to Hopper followed by all the other ants who overthrew the grasshoppers!

It shows us the power of unity; to all become like Flik, and courageously step into our power and say 'NO' to the bullies. There is no ethical or moral reason why anyone should work tirelessly to support a bunch of bureaucrats. There has been massive resistance out there, building up across the world since 2020, which can be seen on alternative platforms, but not mainstream TV… hmmm.

The perpetrators greatest fear is the strength of the human spirit, our resiliency and infinite ability to love. They want us to forget our own power, our divine spark, because when we truly realise and access it - we are untouchable.

The emphasis on net zero climate change is also ramping up. Has anyone in the Green Party movement cottoned on yet that we are the carbon they want rid of? Yes, of course there is natural climate change which is cyclical, however, we are not the cause of the engineered 'fake' climate change to create more taxes for us to pay… etc.

We (the people) are not the ones modifying and manipulating the weather, polluting the skies with chemtrails and heavy metals, poisoning our water with fluoride, oestrogens, pharmaceuticals and more heavy metals; genetically modifying our crops and food, contaminating our soil with the indiscriminate use of glyphosate, herbicides, pesticides, insecticides and fungicides and forcing farmers to use them.

We are not the ones producing synthetic, fake, genetically-modified foods and supplements that our livers do not recognise, cannot assimilate, and make us sick. We are not the ones who have, for decades, been injecting uninformed adults and innocent children with toxic harmful substances that compromise their already compromised immune systems - caused by all of the above!! They are blaming us for their atrocities and destruction on the human population and we are paying the price on many levels for their heinous crimes and greed through our decline in spiritual, mental and physical health and wealth.  Are they not the drug pushers, the sex offenders, the human traffickers, the money launderers? Turn everything 180 degrees - then you will get to the truth!

How can these perpetrators - those at the top, ruling the governments, the big corporations, the banking, education, medical, and judiciary systems etc., be held responsible, accountable and brought to justice? Why have they never been prosecuted and jailed for their crimes against humanity? How have they continually evaded prosecution?

Free energy, clean air and water is already possible and all of the above is reversible. Return all the cathedrals and churches back into energy frequency healing buildings as they once were. Of course, this would not be profitable for the perpetrators at the top, so it is vehemently suppressed. Also, if everyone is happy, healthy, and self-sufficient within our own towns and communities, the perpetrators would lose their power and control over us.

Julie

The continuous flow of cash through the economy is vital to help slow this scary progression toward a digital dystopian, technocratic, transhumanist future that many are sleepwalking into, ultimately making us all completely reliant on a computerised world with no autonomy, privacy or freedom. Cash is independence and gives us the power to transact when and with whom we want. Use cash at local shops and farmers markets and stop using the supermarkets who have the monopoly. Of course, it's not as convenient as Apple Pay but what price is our privacy and freedom worth? It doesn't matter who you vote for - political choice is an illusion - the goal is total digitisation. If this is achieved, the game is over and we will become total slaves. We need to say 'NO' to digital IDs and CBDCs.

Over five years on, I am still living with my sister and brother-in-law. Life is much easier now. The last two years we've had some lovely happy times, family celebrations and parties. On the surface everything seems 'normal' again.

I am so very grateful to my daughters that together we preserved the powerful bond of love between us, and so very thankful that bond was stronger than any outside attempt to destroy it. One daughter has already moved to the West Country and the other is starting the process, which is such wonderful news and will make it so much easier to visit each other more often…woohoo!

Since the start of this year (2025) I am feeling lighter and more optimistic about the future. Although I'm still not sure how I will move on from here, my immediate goals are to improve my mental and physical health, endeavour to live in the present moment, and continue to seek authentic caring relationships.

I resumed karate lessons in January which I am really enjoying, however it has highlighted just how unfit I am! I picked up where I left off over three decades ago and attained my purple/white stripe belt just before my 70th birthday in July.

My daughters treated me to a wonderful holiday with them exploring the Cathar region of Languedoc and visiting the cities of Beziers, Carcassonne and Montpelier. The procedure at both Bristol and Beziers airports went smoothly and the whole experience was surprisingly seamless and a pleasure.

I'm also looking forward to using a birthday gift token to book a flying lesson very soon too!

I remain a conspiracy theorist (haha!) and will continue to question everything and peacefully not comply to any restrictions on my rights, privacy and freedom.

I can only trust that with the help of the powerful light frequencies now flooding the ether, love and goodness will prevail and that we will find the courage to stand up together for our natural inalienable and neuro-cognitive rights. Did you know that whenever you register anything: your children, your car, etc., you give away your right of ownership?

Julie

It seems that we all have been deceived and lied to for decades, and maybe even centuries, which may be hard for many of us to believe. There is some truth in the saying: 'How easy it is to make people believe a lie and how hard it is to undo that lie again'. We have a lot of work ahead!

And in the famous words of the young but insightful poet Percy Byssche Shelley who was obviously 'in the know' even in the early 1800s:

'Rise like Lions after slumber
In unvanquishable number
Shake your chains to earth like dew
Which in sleep had fallen on you
Ye are many - they are few'

Astrology
'the language of probability'

Right now we are in the middle of the shift from the Age of Pisces into the Age of Aquarius; we can feel and see the energetic affects, an exciting time of Change!

I mainly listen to the wonderful Pam Gregory and here are some snippets and forecasts I have heard her talk about; also included are comments from other astrologers and a few of my own observations and views.

One of the main themes I have heard being discussed over the last months is all about 'Change' and 'Revolution' - not pitchforks and violence, but how we, as a collective, are shifting from the age of 'topdown rule' to the age of rule from the 'grassroots up'... i.e. the power is shifting back to the people - it is our time to shape the world into a better place. We have choices and the time for the 'Revolution of Choice' is now.

Transformational years until 2034 - what an amazing opportunity we have!

Astrology shows us that the global systems are changing in tandem with rising consciousness, and there will be unexpected changes in world leadership. Nothing is really as it seems or as we've always believed.

We are experiencing transformational energy - no matter how bad things can look in one moment, they can change quickly, and over the next years, more and more people will question the narrative, and remember our position in the Universe, not just who we are on Earth. We will understand that we're not just beings on Earth, we're much more galactically orientated, and galactic beings around us are cheering us on.

Within this transition time:

Everything is Energy - more people being bold - AUTHENTICITY - physical health a priority - people feeling squashed globally - healing - year of reckoning - development in aviation - power outages - LOVE - new fertile land emerging - energy is becoming magnetic so pay attention to what you focus on - big financial change - less polution in the earth - satellite technology - UNITY - change in economy - recognition of our energetic sovereignty - turbulence this year - PEACE - shedding limited beliefs - increasing seismic activity - underwater volcanoes - changes in land mass - earth upgrading - expanding consciousness - equality - radar - photography - global awareness - ancient civilisations were way ahead of us - TRUTH - justice - pioneers - angelic support - wind and solar incompatible with old power grids - collective well-being - manifestation - veil thinning - actions have consequences for the whole - GRATITUDE - true potential - new paradigms - turbulence next year - intuition - technology innovation - spirituality - more extreme weather - earth electrified - LIGHT - we are going to a way better place - less toxicity in the earth - collaboration - move to magnetism as our source of power, rather than electricity which will give us free energy across the world - FORGIVENESS - being open to new possibilities - barefoot on the grass - adapting to change - contributing to a more harmonious world - intensity - BREATH unity consciousness - WATER - nature - galactic support - shifting from a focus on material possessions to a more spiritual and purpose-driven life - rise in consciousness - power of now fast change ahead - oneness - indigeonous prophecies - remembrance - **Everything is Connected**

'Heart energy is the Currency of the Future'

'Everything is a Choice'

'Choose to be kind to others and to yourself'

Joe

Me - in 2013 when one of my influencers, favourite singer-songwriters was Matt Bellamy from the band 'Muse'. Looking back at these lyrics now, after the last few years, they take on a new meaning...

Joe

Paranoia is in bloom
The PR transmissions will resume
They'll try to push drugs that keep us all dumbed down
And hope that we will never see the truth around

Another promise, another scene
Another packaged lie to keep us trapped in greed
And all the green belts wrapped around our minds
And endless red tape to keep the truth confined

They will not force us
They will stop degrading us
They will not control us
We will be victorious

Interchanging mind control
Come, let the revolution take its toll
If you could flick the switch and open your third eye
You'd see that we should never be afraid to die

Rise up and take the power back
It's time the fat cats had a heart attack
You know that their time's coming to an end
We have to unify and watch our flag ascend

'Uprising' by Muse, from their album
'The Resistance' 2009

Conclusion

As this book concludes and we head into the autumn of 2025, I believe that in a couple of years we will be looking at a very different world and it will just keep getting better.

Since we emerged from 2020, the changes I, and many have wanted to see, are happening much quicker now. You won't see any of it on the nightly news or in the newspapers, but it's happening. Everything is speeding up.

Six years ago, the entire world closed down because of a 'high consequence infectious disease'. Looking back at previous books, it is fascinating to read the stories… In Book 1, all the writers describing their initial reactions to the Lockdowns when no-one really knew what was going on, and there was a lot of fear. Reading on through books 2 and 3, there are so many interesting views and opinions.

Conclusion

Some say the pandemic was a virus, and others say it was media manipulation and government propaganda. Some say it was a bit of both. Whatever your view is, the emergency powers which were introduced were intended to control every aspect of our lives.

Some considered the emergency rules were an overreaction by the government and did not comply, whilst others thought the rules weren't strict enough.

Did the governments across the world do the best they could with the information they had at the time? Should it have been less or more strict? I wonder what you thought at the time... and, looking back, what do you think now?

I focus on the world I want to see...the old rulers going, because they don't serve us, and new Leaders taking their place, leading with love, respect and by example, leading from the heart and doing what is best for the people. I see people living in peace and abundance, I see justice, happiness and love, fairness and integrity, a place where it is impossible to think of hurting another living being. That's the world I see... and what we think, say and focus on is what we create, so imagine how powerful we are becoming with the number of people across the world who are now focussing on only the good. Our Focus is our Superpower. Collectively we are Strong. We each chose to be here at this time and so we may as well make the most of it!

It doesn't mean I'm not deeply affected by the horrors and suffering that are still taking place in our world, and I care and pray every day for the people who find themselves living in it through no choice of their own.

I see us in the transition, all at different stages, all to be respected. Many have been rebuilding for a long time, using unlimited creativity and innovation, creating wonderful new ways of living and working, cleaning up our world and making it a beautiful place to live in. Some are already living it, and for some it's just around the corner. Others do not believe our world can transition into something wonderful from the chaos, division and hatred. Time to choose our Frequency!

Keep Shining Your Light, We Are All Connected, Trust Your Intuition, and Take a Leap Of Faith as we step into unknown territory, and collectively 'Let's Make This World A Better Place.'
BE KIND!

Forever Positive and optimistic ● See you next year and remember... *'we don't all see things the same way!'*

'The best way to predict the future is to create it'

'WE are the change'

Conclusion

Thank you to all my wonderful writers who have joined me in this book, and if you would like to join me to share your story in Book 5, please contact me via the website **www.memoriesoflockdown.com**

I'd love to hear from you if you wish to tell your story through the Lockdown years, or maybe you just want to share a short story about something that happened to you during these times as a direct result of the changes brought about by the Lockdowns. All our stories are interesting and unique, and in many ways will be quite unbelievable when read ten years from now!

Do You Remember?

Back in 2021, I wrote in my introduction 'the world is in crisis and we need Unity, Trust and Love, not Division, Hopelessness and Fear'. I still believe this, and in 2025 we see the world continuing through chaotic times. We are absolutely in a fight for our freedom. Every country in the world is facing difficulty right now, and the positive side of this is that this is connecting people across the world as never before.

I see division being created and advertised daily through the TV and every other media outlet, for those who choose to watch and listen. Division - Divide and Conquer.

Divided we were... by our different views on masks and vaccines, 'Eating Out to Help Out' one minute, and finding ourselves in a second lockdown the next, whch extended over the Christmas of 2021. People died alone in hospitals. Family members were denied the right to sit beside their loved ones in care homes which became like prisons. Small businesses shut down and many never recovered. Families and neighbours turned against each other and fear became the number one weapon.

Two years of education was stolen from our children. Do you remember the blue tape around playgrounds, zoom classrooms, fear, isolation and confusion. A rise in mental health issues, self-harm, suicide and eating disorders are consistently reported. We were told to protect the NHS and Granny, while those who made the rules did exactly what they liked. They had parties, flew around the world, handed out billion-dollar contracts to friends and the rich became richer.
All to 'keep us safe'.

Do You Remember?

Was it madness to lock the world down? It is now clear that more damage was done by the lockdowns than by the virus, which some believe was highly infectious, and others believe was a winter flu. If another 'highly infectious virus' is announced, I wonder how many people would be willing to live in isolation and go into another world lockdown.

Was covid-19 a deadly virus or was it the biggest crime against humanity the world has ever seen.

What do you think?

Topics being discussed as we go to print at the beginning of October 2025

AI - Immigration - Digital ID - Cost of Living - Farmers under attack - Integrity - Freedom Of Speech - Asylum Hotels - LOVE - The Bible - Lawful - Net Zero - Grooming Gangs in UK - Turbo Cancer - Legal - Human Trafficking - Autonomy - Kindness - Conspiracy Theorists - Balance - Soul Choice - Israel - Vaccines Promoted - Vaccine Damage - Trolls - War - Climate Change - Education - Hospitals - What's Council Tax really paying for - Off-Worlders - Divinely Guided - Compassion - Discernment - Men in Women's Sports - CBDC - Mental Health - Fear - for your safety - Hidden in Plain Sight - Defibrillator - Crime - Technology - Child Trafficking - Spiritually Protected - Gold - Heart Attacks - Gaza - Joy - The Age of Aquarius - for your Protection - Cameras in Supermarkets - New Earth - Not Safe and Effective - Food Shortages - Solar Panel Farms - Organic Food - Bitcoin - NHS - Awakening - Harmony - God's Earth - Frequency Energy Healing - Demonetised - Happiness - Utility Bills - The Galactic Council - Deep State - Med Beds - UFOs

- Palestine - Coercion - Consciousness - Economy - New Earth - The Environment - Manipulation - Identify As - Housing - Walk-Ins - Landgrab - Controlled Opposition - Belief - Elementals - Gratitude - Ivermectin - Employment - Lockdowns in Schools - Hate Speech - Beauty - Federation of Light - Transhumanism - Corruption - Shill - Timelines - Respect - Interdimensional - Detox - Eugenics - Confidence - Ukraine - Peace - Robots - Sex Education in Primary Schools - Financial Insecurity - Sadness - Trust - Sovereign Being - Silver - Fake Meat - Dimming the Sun - LGBTQ++ - Net Zero - Chemtrails - Deceipt - Humility - Hormone Blocking - Social Media - the bigger picture - Cloud Seeding - Censorship - Cameras on Roads - Cash Is King - Hope - Blood Clots - Non Binary - Good Vs Evil - Dimensions - Fluoride - Facism - Crystals - Eating Bugs - Courage - Myocarditis - Right Wing Extremist - Side Effects - Magic - Russia - Energy - Harmful Content - Protection - Higher Self - Health Insecurity - The Golden Age - Governments in chaos - Trump Derangement Syndrome - Mother Earth - Solar Panel Farms - Wisdom - Nicotine - Anti-Semitism - Food Shortages - Men in Women's Toilets - Misinformation - Card Only - Cashless Society - What is a Woman? - Forgiveness - Light Vs Dark - Died Suddenly - Methylene Blue - Islamophobia - New Variant - Galactic Family - smoke and mirrors - the shooting of Charlie Kirk, USA - 'Unite the Kingdom' Rally in London - 'Operation Raise the Colours' - Interstellar Traveller 3I/Atlas - Comet or Spaceship? - 30 arrests a day in the UK over offensive posts on social media - Trump's UK State visit, and so much more...

*'When we look back on this time,
all that will really have mattered
is how we treated each other'*

www.ingramcontent.com/pod-product-compliance
Lightning Source LLC
Chambersburg PA
CBHW040303170426
43194CB00021B/2875